The Art of the Pose

Heather Marcovitch

The Art of the Pose

Oscar Wilde's Performance Theory

PETER LANG
Bern · Berlin · Bruxelles · Frankfurt am Main · New York · Oxford · Wien

Bibliographic information published by Die Deutsche Bibliothek
Die Deutsche Bibliothek lists this publication in the Deutsche Nationalbibliografie; detailed bibliographic data is available on the Internet at ‹http://dnb.ddb.de›.

British Library Cataloguing-in-Publication Data: A catalogue record for this book is available from *The British Library*, Great Britain

Library of Congress Cataloging-in-Publication Data

Marcovitch, Heather, 1969-
The art of the pose : Oscar Wilde's performance theory / Heather Marcovitch.
p. cm.
Includes bibliographical references.
ISBN 978-3-0343-0439-9
1. Wilde, Oscar, 1854-1900–Criticism and interpretation. 2. Wilde, Oscar, 1854-1900–Knowledge–Performing arts. 3. Wilde, Oscar, 1854-1900–Aesthetics. 4. Wilde, Oscar, 1854–1900–Philosophy. 5. Self-presentation in literature. 6. Self in literature. 7. Identity (Philosophical concept) in literature. 8. Persona (Psychoanalysis) 9. Image (Philosophy) I. Title.
PR5827.A35M37 2010
828'.809–dc22

2010033903

Cover illustration: Oliver Paque (William Henry Pike), 'Daily Paragraph' 1890, Mary Evans Picture Library

Cover design: Thomas Jaberg, Peter Lang AG

ISBN 978-3-0343-0439-9

Hochfeldstrasse 32, CH-3012 Bern, Switzerland
info@peterlang.com, www.peterlang.com, www.peterlang.net

Printed in Switzerland

Table of Contents

List of Figures

Acknowledgements

I would like to thank Chris Snodgrass for his sound advice and mentorship during the early incarnation of this book. His words about writing and scholarship have shaped my work more than he can realize. Profuse thanks also to Pamela Gilbert, Alistair Duckworth, and Ralf Remshardt for their wise comments about my work, Oscar Wilde, and the many other aspects of both late-Victorian England and about performance studies that have found their way into these pages.

Research for this book was conducted partly at the William Andrews Clark Memorial Library at UCLA. Thanks to Suzanne Tatian and Jennifer Schaffner for their help in showing me some of the obscure documents that can make research so rewarding. Also, to Scott Jacobs for his help with locating and sending me the images that are reproduced in this book.

Katrin Forrer of Peter Lang provided me with editorial advice and support and for that I am grateful. Daniela Christen, formerly of Peter Lang, guided me through the initial stages of the publication process.

My colleagues at Red Deer College have provided me with a great deal of support in the late stages of writing this book. Torben Andersen, Jane MacNeil and Pam Clarke were especially instrumental in helping me secure resources for the final revisions. My students in my various Victorian Literature classes gave me an opportunity to refine my thoughts.

On a personal note, I need to acknowledge that I owe a lot of the fortitude it took to see this project through – especially during the many upheavals and changes in my life– to certain people. Special thanks to Larry Steinbrenner for his support during the more stressful times. Thanks also to Carlen Lavigne for her patience and her willingness to listen to sudden brainstorms. To Nick and Tina Melczarek for bringing feather boas to crucial events and for unwavering support. And many thanks to Kristen Chancey for some of the most entertaining and informative conversations about the nineteenth century I will ever have and for helping me flesh out some of the early ideas in this book.

And to my family, who is always there, regardless of wherever I might be.

This book truly began with the initial help of the Edwin C. And Mary Neal Kirkland Travel Grant from the University of Florida. I have been able to finish it with funding from a Special Projects Grant from Red Deer College.

Introduction
Oscar Wilde and Performance Theory

Oscar Wilde was a man of the theatre. The statement sounds obvious, given his renown as a playwright, but, for Wilde, the theatre was more than just a venue for his plays. His writings, both dramatic and non-dramatic, are full of meditations about the theatre and more specifically about his fascination with acting. During the period in the 1880s when Wilde was a working journalist, he published many theatrical reviews; his acquaintanceships with the famous actors of the time such as Ellen Terry, Modjeska (he translated a poem of hers), Henry Irving, and especially Sarah Bernhardt and Lillie Langtry helped to define his public image when he was beginning his career in London. The doomed Sibyl Vane in *The Picture of Dorian Gray* is, of course, an actress, the Canterville Ghost delights in scaring the American tenants of his ancestral home by staging elaborate theatrical tableaux, and his short story 'The Model Millionaire' might not involve an actor, but the title character is a fairly successful impersonator. Among his full-length critical essays is not only his analysis of Shakespearean costume in 'The Truth of Masks' but the telling quote in 'The Portrait of Mr. W.H.' which states that 'all Art [is] to some degree a mode of acting, an attempt to realise one's own personality on some imaginative plane out of reach of the trammelling accidents and limitations of real life.'[1]

This quote links Wilde's interest in the theatrical world and particularly in the nature of performing to his aesthetics, his forays into decadent and symbolist writing, his Hegelian theories, his

1 Oscar Wilde, 'The Portrait of Mr. W.H.,' in *The Soul of Man under Socialism and Selected Critical Prose*, ed. Linda Dowling, 31–101 (London: Penguin, 2001), 33.

public image, as well as more obviously his plays. Performance to Wilde is not merely an occasional subject matter, nor a campy mode of expression. Wilde, for all of his entertaining wit, had been interested in the question of performance and its relationship both to concepts of identity and ways of being in the world since he was a university student. It was a fitting concern of his: always the outsider in his world, whether as an Irishman living in England, a middle-class writer friendly with the upper classes, an artist in a Philistine environment, and a gay man who was also married, Wilde was always interested in the way the self could and often needed to be manipulated in order to engage with one's culture. The self, he argued, was neither as authentic nor as integrated as was believed; rather, an individual's identity stems from a series of cultivated performances where moods and influences are absorbed into his or her dress, behaviour, thoughts, and experiences.

The artists and writers of the 1890s were fascinated by performance, both the act and the individuals who excelled at it. This fascination is expressed by poets of the English decadence such as Arthur Symons, whose poems about music halls and their performers caused a sensation, and essayists like Max Beerbohm enthusiastically championing the artificial. Dancers such as Loïe Fuller and Jane Avril were painted by Toulouse-Lautrec, and actors were household names, their cultural importance epitomized in Henry Irving's knighthood in 1895, the first actor ever to be awarded one. In the mid-nineteenth century, the visual arts had men like John Ruskin and Walter Pater articulate a poetics to better appreciate and interpret art; in the latter decades of the nineteenth century, performance had Oscar Wilde. His body of work fuses performance with art, morality and the concept of the self into a theory which accounts for both performance as a mode of action and its more static, existential offshoot, persona. Wilde's writings offer the *fin de siècle* a model for the artists of that period to articulate their ideas of performance.

Performance is the theoretical paradigm which structures Wilde's writing, and its development can be traced through a chronological look at his works. He is influenced by a wide range of philosophers, scientists, and sages, such as John Ruskin and Walter Pater, and especially by Pater's Preface and notorious Conclusion to *The Renaissance*. Pater's emphasis on the value of increasing one's experiences and the importance of developing one's personality in order to heighten these experiences was refined by Wilde into the idea of developing one's personality in order to give a better performance so as to engage more fully with the world. In fact, for Wilde the performance and the self are inseparable; seeing a performance as the art of the self, he argues in his writings that through this seemingly artificial mode of being one can paradoxically lead a more authentic life. One can also, following Ruskin, achieve that element of greatness which Ruskin believes is a manifestation of the divine in mundane existence. Ruskin states that greatness in art is that 'which conveys to the spectator, by any means whatsoever, the greatest number of the greatest ideas.'[2] Substitute the paintings Ruskin has in mind with the human being whose everyday behaviour can be refined into a work of art, and one finds the seed of Wilde's conception of performance. It is not merely an artificial form of play but a method by which one introduces great ideas into one's culture.

Although the idea of what is in part the performance of everyday life is not new (one can only look to Shakespeare's dramas to see this notion in play), what Wilde was doing was providing the examples from which modern performance theorists later drew on to elucidate the field of performance studies, mostly a mixture of phenomenology, theatre studies and anthropological work, although it has in recent years embraced theoretical work from other disciplines. Wilde's work is nascent performance theory, slightly

2 John Ruskin, *The Genius of John Ruskin: Selections from His Writings*, ed. John D. Rosenberg (New York: George Brazillier, 1963), 22.

predating the early work in this field done by Russian acting teachers like Konstantin Stanislavski and Michael Chekhov. Wilde's work also resonates with writers who do not reference him directly, such as sociologist Erving Goffman in his important work *The Performance of Everyday Life* and Richard Schechner's seminal work on theorizing performance, as well as with performance theorists such as Marvin Carlson who use Wilde as an example of the complexities in a performance of everyday life. For all of these writers, and for Wilde as well, performance is not simply a prescribed way of behaving under certain theatrical conditions, nor is it merely a self-conscious awareness of one's own everyday behaviour. Performance is a discursive field where notions of identity, art, culture and social relations are interrogated and through which one becomes an active participant in one's culture.

Wilde is interested in the poetics of performance and indeed devotes a large part of his writings to elaborating upon what transforms the self into a performance and thereby into a work of art. In this, he follows Pater's contention that experience 'is ringed round for each one of us by that thick wall of personality through which no real voice has ever pierced on its way to us'.[3] Wilde believes that all people are essentially egoists and that the development of one's performance is not only crucial to understanding the self, but is the only way to prevent egoism from deteriorating into solipsism. This is why, for Wilde, the development of the performing self is the development of the critical spirit that both Pater and Matthew Arnold insist is a necessary component of existing within modern culture. In 'The Critic as Artist,' Gilbert says:

> It seems to me that with the development of the critical spirit we shall be able to realise, not merely our own lives, but the collective life of the race, and so

---

3 Walter Pater, *The Renaissance: Studies in Art and Poetry. The 1893 Text*, ed. Donald L. Hill (Berkeley and Los Angeles: University of California Press, 1980), 187.

> to make ourselves absolutely modern, in the true meaning of the word modernity.[4]

To perform the self, one must develop a critical awareness of oneself and, through that, a critical awareness of one's culture and society. For Wilde then what is equally important to becoming aware of oneself as potentially art is an understanding of the mechanisms and limitations involved in cultivating oneself in this fashion.

The poetics of the performance of the self, according to Wilde, are disarmingly simple: assume and always be conscious of one's inherent fragmentary nature, cultivate each fragment to the best of its artistic possibilities, and do so under the rubric of a secular morality that stresses compassion and community with others. Above all, never succumb to the cheap stereotypes that a commodity culture utilizes voraciously in order to create marketable images. In other words, the self as work of art should strive to be unique and deeply felt, rather than, cynically or weakly, be a pale copy of another's performance. The latter dictum is one that especially concerned Wilde. In his early writing career, he had to contend with both the British and the American periodicals' cruel caricatures of both his public image and his pronouncements on aesthetics. The Victorian periodical press becomes a bit of a monolithic antagonist to Wilde, despite the appearance of sympathetic reviews and articles and despite Wilde's own work as a newspaper writer. (My use of the term 'the press' refers to the many conservative publications that seemed nearly united in their disapprobation of Wilde.)

In his later writings, he warned of the danger of relinquishing control of one's performance, both to the integrity of the self and of society as a whole. An individual performance shaped and realized by that individual does more than develop the self; it also challenges

---

4 Oscar Wilde, 'The Critic as Artist,' in *The Soul of Man under Socialism and Selected Critical Prose*, ed. Linda Dowling, 213–279 (London: Penguin, 2001), 254.

society's pressure on individuals to conform to an already-established social type. Because Wilde sees the potential for subversion in performance (and, in 'The Soul of Man under Socialism' even suggests its revolutionary possibilities), he is also aware of the potential harm it can do if not cultivated with care, and his writings of the 1890s are concerned with just that.

Wilde's work on performance goes by different names: realizing the self, cultivating one's personality, developing the critical spirit. All of these terms are interconnected, all recur throughout his writings, and all have traditionally been linked with Wilde's own status as a celebrity in late-Victorian culture – and even beyond, for writers looking back at the period, such as Richard le Gallienne, note that the 1890s was a decade where it seemed as if anyone who had any personal connection to a celebrity claimed that status for themselves. Le Gallienne writes (without including himself in this criticism, apparently): 'There was a vulgar exploitation of minor personalities. The era of the engineered boom was beginning, and one had a feeling that men were getting "famous" too quickly.'[5] Osbert Burdett, looking back on the end of the nineteenth century, writes that 'the typical attitude . . . was one of preoccupation with the public, a public no less courted than despised.'[6] Burdett is referring to the 1890s as well (and to Whistler in particular), but it is worth noting that Wilde was not only one of the most notable celebrities of this time but that he anticipated the preoccupation with celebrity in the 1890s by using his own celebrity as a dialectic in the previous decades. While still a student at Oxford, Wilde's remarks were picked up by a London periodical; as a minor celebrity in London, his picture was on collectible postcards, his image was used to sell items as different as ice cream and cigars, and he was the

5 Richard Le Gallienne, *The Romantic '90s* (New York: Doubleday Page, 1926), 13.

6 Osbert Burdett, *The Beardsley Period: An Essay in Perspective* (London: Bodley Head, 1925), 7–8.

subject of a celebrity impersonator who was a fixture in the music halls. In a more satirical light, his image was not only the subject of countless caricatures, but also helped to sell satirical songsheets so that the songs could be learned and played in the home. Regenia Gagnier and the scholars who have followed her have already noted that, rather than eschewing this commodification of his public image, Wilde was an active participant in his own self-marketing; as a result, Gagnier argues, one needs to reread Wilde's work in light of the commodity culture he was engaging in.[7] I do not dispute this way of reading Wilde, but what I mean to argue in this study is that Wilde's relationship to performance involves a dialectic (which at times lays itself bare as a tense struggle) between performing within a commodity culture which did reward Wilde financially and eventually with a literary reputation and his work on performance as a structural paradigm which Wilde believed ought to subvert that same culture. In addition, Wilde's work on performance has been underexamined and this has been an oversight in the field.

What is needed is to position Wilde as an early writer of performance theory and thereby to extend performance theory into literary studies, with which it currently has more of a tangential relationship. Modern performance studies, such as the work that has been done by theatre scholars and directors like Richard Schechner and anthropologists like Victor Turner, assumes a link between modern theatrical performances and the performance-based rituals of tribal cultures. These writers posit that performance is the method by which individuals become social beings; in modern performances, it also serves as an expression for normally-unarticulated anxieties about one's existence as a social being. Performance is distinguished from the performative, that term that has replaced sociologist Erving Goffman's phrase 'the performance of everyday

---

7 See Regenia Gagnier, *Idylls of the Marketplace: Oscar Wilde and the Victorian Public* (Stanford: Stanford University Press, 1986).

life' by the awareness of the theatricality in one's behaviour; the performative, however, is an aspect of performance and sometimes the distinction between the two terms is blurred.[8]

According to Schechner, performance originally involved the transmission of certain culturally-accepted codes, such as in the ritualized performances of shamans or in the performance of religious ceremonies. Schechner claims that it was the Ancient Greeks who first separated performance from a direct signifier of its culture to a more abstract symbol. 'Historically speaking, in the West,' he argues, 'drama detached itself from doing. Communication replaced manifestation.'[9] Instead of a performance enacting the exchange of goods (meat, for instance) between houses, it would symbolize either the idea of exchange or, with the advent of modern drama in the late nineteenth century, the emotional or psychological impact of the exchange. Schechner writes:

> This convergence of symbolic and actual event [present in the exchange of a good] is missing from aesthetic theatre. We have sought for it by trying to make the performer 'responsible' or 'visible' in and for his performance – either through psychodramatic techniques or other psychological means.[10]

Schechner locates the performer as the vehicle through which the participants (both performers and audience members) try to recover the loss of the original signified of the performance, that concrete meaning which was obscured when performance became symbolic. This argument is echoed by Bert States in reference to modern drama. States sees what he calls a 'double consciousness' in a per-

8 Both J.L. Austin's work on performative speech and Judith Butler's work on the performative in gender behaviour are examples of the overlap between the performative and performance.

9 Richard Schechner, *Essays on Performance Theory 1970–1976* (New York: Drama Book Specialists, 1977), 38.

10 Ibid., 73.

formance; in an effective performance, one sees the mechanisms utilized by the actor even as one suspends one's disbelief in order to appreciate the drama being performed. For States, the performer is never 'lost' within a role, but he or she provides, through the use of his or her body, an additional text to be read into the performance. This way of seeing the performer is a method that dates back to the early twentieth century where, according to Philip Auslander,

> Theorists as diverse as Stanislavski, Brecht, and Grotowski all implicitly designate the actor's self as the *logos* of performance, all assume that the actor's self precedes and grounds her performance and that it is the presence of this self in performance that provides the audience with access to human truths.[11]

States argues that a dramatic performance is motivated by a kind of theatrical shorthand, where characters represent easily-identifiable concepts that stand in for the purported complexities of the characters. 'Even a character as philosophical as Hamlet,' States writes,

> can hardly be called a profound thinker on the evidence of his thoughts. Any one of them might serve as the epigraph for an entire philosophy of existence or ethical responsibility, but we never catch him tracking an idea that does not cast his whole being (and hence the actor's) into a visible attitude. In short, philosophy, in the theater, must unfold itself, literally, as a thinking of the body.[12]

Performance therefore is comprised of a dynamic relationship between text and body, the body becoming a sign to the public which economically substitutes for the entire personality. This *persona* is the self as bodily text or, as Auslander puts it, 'a textual entity generated

---

11 Philip Auslander, *From Acting to Performance: Essays in Modernism and Postmodernism* (New York: Routledge, 1997), 30.

12 Bert O. States, *Great Reckonings in Little Rooms: On the Phenomenology of Theater* (Berkeley: University of California Press, 1987), 133.

by the performance context.'[13] The persona is an integral part of Wilde's writings about performance and serves as the point where Wilde's writings are refracted and doubled by his own performances, from the aesthete to the sophisticate to the social outcast, bearing strong similarities to States' description of a theatrical shorthand. In fact, Wilde's various personae form images so resonant with both the Victorian and our contemporary public that one reads his works always having an additional character, 'Oscar Wilde,' as an integral part of the text.

But while performance involves negotiating between text and body, or between self and persona, it obviously does not take place without the presence of some sort of audience. This not only marks performance as social but also marks its extension beyond a narcissistic obsession with ways of portraying oneself. If Schechner argues that modern performance is a distilled version of older ritualistic behaviours, Victor Turner sees culture as a series of different, competing performances, often operating in antagonistic relationships to each other. Turner recognizes two types of performances within cultures: the performance which reinforces the social hierarchy (which he refers to as 'structure'), and the performance of individuals marginalized by the same hierarchy (referred to as *communitas*). Structure, according to Turner, distances individuals from each other by locking them into statuses and roles and what he also refers to as personae, in this case 'the role-mask, not the unique individual.'[14] For Turner, the history of cultures can be read as an ongoing tension between structure and communitas, which he defines as being essentially an iconoclastic, subversive performance. 'Communitas,' he writes, 'does not merge identities; it liberates them

13 Auslander, *From Acting to Performance*, 44.

14 Victor Turner, *Dramas, Fields, and Metaphors: Symbolic Action in Human Society* (Ithaca and London: Cornell University Press, 1974), 237.

from conformity to general norms.'[15] Within this tension, though, Turner sees communication and change as possible through movement which will eventually see the subversive become the normative. His term *liminality* describes a state which he marks as a transition between the anti-structure of communitas and the structure of the social norm and the accompanying 'liminal' figures – people, such as artists or performers, who are able to move between the two groups.[16]

Turner's model for social behaviour is strikingly similar to one that Wilde uses in his writings. Calling himself an iconoclast and embedding sharp social criticisms in his writings, even his aesthetic ones, Wilde partly champions performance as a way of developing an idea of communitas among marginalized individuals. A unique and personal performance, in his view, opens up a social space that has the potential to subvert the social stereotypes and the norms that inform them. It is a fairly easy move for Wilde to make, since, as Andrew Parker and Eve Kosofsky Sedgwick point out, 'the performative has . . . been from its inception already infected with queerness.'[17] A performance, recognized as being an artificial mode of behaviour, calls attention to the artificiality involved in behaving according to social norms and the subversive potential that shadows every norm, a point Wilde gleefully makes in *The Importance of Being Earnest*; exchanging these performances with other individuals can lead to the development of a subculture. Wilde's extension of performance into communitas produced some interesting results, from the American playwright Clyde Fitch who enthusiastically proclaimed his belief in the existence of Willie Hughes, the fictional character in 'The Portrait of Mr. W.H.,' to the reports of the group

15 Ibid., 274.

16 Ibid., 273.

17 Andrew Parker and Eve Kosofsky Sedgwick, 'Introduction to *Performativity and Performance*,' in *The Performance Studies Reader*, ed. Henry Bial, 167–174 (New York Routledge: 2004), 169.

of young men who attended the premiere of *Lady Windermere's Fan* sporting green carnations in their buttonholes, to Wilde's final poem *The Ballad of Reading Gaol*, which forms communitas out of a group of outcast prisoners through their witnessing the performance of a man condemned to die.

Thus performance, far from being strictly a solipsistic act, is the realization that one's self is always already constructed through one's relationship to others. It is the self not necessarily constructed inside the boundaries of social laws, but one which, through its relationship to other distinct performances, creates identities which can use their alterity as a way of challenging or subverting the social order. Jonathan Dollimore sees this move as being essentially transgressive insofar as a performance is inseparable from subversive or deviant desires and, as a result, 'actually decentres or disperses the self' – in this case, into different performances.[18] In the cultivation of performance, one is looking outward from oneself, so to speak, but one also has an external perspective, seeing one's performance in the context of other performances. It is at the juncture of these two perspectives from which Wilde writes.

This book charts the development of Wilde's theories of performance and its more aesthetically-based variant, the persona. For Wilde, performance and persona are intertwined and he often describes an individual's persona – the image of the self put forth to the public – as the most fundamental type of performance. Wilde's work on persona, with its connections to image and identity, resonates with the psychoanalytic approaches to the self that began to gain some currency in the *fin de siècle*. His work may predate most of Freud's major writings, but he too is aware of the pleasurable and anxiety-ridden forces that govern the self and he sees a persona as created out of the tension between these forces. Whereas his earlier

18 Jonathan Dollimore, *Sexual Dissidence: Augustine to Wilde, Freud to Foucault* (Oxford: Clarendon Press, 1991), 14.

work is concerned with developing the concepts of performance and persona as largely positivist methods of engaging with the world, his work of the 1890s shows a clear anxiety about the potential destructiveness of an unmediated persona.

A note on the terminology in this book: *Persona* is a word I use frequently in this study to refer to Wilde's theories; it is not Wilde's term, as he prefers to use the term *personality* in his critical essays. But in my view, the word *persona* emphasizes the connections to both Wilde's aesthetics and to performance. It stresses that self-conscious detachment that Wilde believes is necessary for the development of the self. And unlike the word *personality*, *persona* does not imply any given correlation between public performance and the interior self. In fact, since Wilde was a Hegelian thinker in many ways, the relationship between public and private selves is contested in his writings.[19] For Wilde, a person is not born a performer but always has the potential to become one; each work of art, as well, is not necessarily a performance, but also has this potential. In this book, I use *performance* when referring to more active behaviour and *persona* when referring to the image the individual projects without any corresponding action on his or her part.

Wilde's own public performances gesture towards dissolving the boundaries between performer and spectator. If his aim is to influence people into a more aesthetic performance of their everyday lives, he is also looking towards creating communitas or what Schechner calls the 'community of participants' that he believes is the key to 'environmental theatre,' a performance which exceeds the boundaries of the traditional stage.[20] Wilde becomes an actor when

19 For discussions of Hegel's influence on Wilde, see Philip E. Smith II and Michael S. Helfand's introduction to *Oscar Wilde's Oxford Notebooks: A Portrait of Mind in the Making* (New York: Oxford University Press, 1989), and Rodney Shewan, *Oscar Wilde: Art and Egotism* (London: Macmillan, 1977), 19.

20 Richard Schechner, *Environmental Theater*, 2nd ed. (New York: Applause, 1994), 245.

he 'plays' himself in public, distancing himself from the traditional humanist concept of the self by structuring his own public displays as performances. In his public discourses on aesthetics, his costumed body offering an implied commentary on his spoken words, he represents States' concept of being, as an actor, 'a kind of storyteller whose specialty is that he *is* the story he is telling.'[21] As both actor and writer, Wilde aims to expand the stage into the world, making his cultural environment theatrical and thus opening up new possibilities in the relationship between the self and its world.

21 States, *Great Reckonings*, 123.

Chapter One
Foundations and Experiments: Oscar Wilde at Oxford

Neither a theory of performance nor a concept of an individual's persona emanated fully-flung from Wilde's head. There was a rather lengthy process of germination, of putting together discrete pieces of a more complex theory, sometimes with a teleology in mind, and sometimes through trial and error. Wilde at Oxford University was immersed in the scholarly world's attempts to reconcile the 'new' evolutionary theories of Darwin with still-popular philosophical idealism, most notably that of Hegel and Hume. The importance of the notebooks Wilde kept while at Oxford from 1874 to 1879 is not that therein lies a nascent theory to be read into all of his works; indeed, the notebooks, like many student notebooks, largely consist of copied quotations from works Wilde was either reading or studying at the time and a smattering of half-formed ideas. But there are certain key thinkers and ideas that never left Wilde's thought and that, in revised forms, become part of the 'critical spirit' lurking behind his poetry, fiction, essays, and dramas.

Smith and Helfand argue in the introduction to their edition of Wilde's Oxford Notebooks for the particular importance of Hegel in shaping Wilde's thought. Indeed, Hegel's dialectic might be the singular most important piece of philosophy Wilde utilizes in his writings. As well, Wilde's exposure to Oxford's Walter Pater's *Studies in the History of the Renaissance* (especially in its tacit argument against Matthew Arnold's ideas about criticism) gave him not only a model for how style can contribute to the meaning of a prose essay but an example of how one can revalue man as a sensational rather than a rational being. There is also a grappling with Herbert Spencer's appropriation of evolutionary theories into the Victorian social sphere which Wilde in his student days tries alternately to incorporate into his own thoughts and to refute. But these are not the only thinkers which influenced Wilde as a university student, nor do they survive intact once Wilde begins to write about performance.

No performance however is possible without the inclusion of the body and it would stand to reason that no theory of performance can be developed strictly on the intellectual plane. If nothing else, Pater's exhortation to include the body in one's experience of life, 'To burn with a hard, gemlike flame' and his sensualised appreciations of Leonardo and Winckelmann in the *Renaissance* stand as an early inclusion of the body into literary criticism. Wilde may not have written extensively on the body while at Oxford, but he began to use his own body – dressing and speaking in certain ways, for example – to begin to think critically about performance. Was he mocking his classmates, fulfilling a need to stand out from the students who were above him in class or just being singular? Some of his former classmates believed that to be so. But again, while his intentions at the time may not have been critically sophisticated, just like his notes may not have been fully developed, Wilde's behaviour at Oxford led to him becoming recognized as a representative 'aesthete' by London magazines such as *Punch*, which indirectly led to Wilde giving his lectures on aestheticism in America, which led to Wilde 'being' the aesthete years before he actually gained fame as a writer.

Wilde's appreciation of performance can likely be traced back to his flamboyant mother Jane Elgee, Lady Wilde, who wrote fiery Irish nationalist poetry under the name Speranza. Richard Ellmann describes Lady Wilde as a woman who invented a romantic Italian ancestry for herself, and who, at the salons she presided over, first in Dublin and then later in London, 'cut a figure in increasingly outlandish costumes, surmounted by headdresses and festooned with outsized and bizarre jewellery,'[1] but who also imparted to her son the sense that a poet ought to be a larger-than-life personality. It is therefore likely that Wilde arrived at Oxford already with a heightened sensitivity about physical performance, the decorating and exhibition of the body, which he never abandoned, despite his clear intellectual prowess, for a more erudite scholarly approach. It is this interest which motivated him to experiment with the effects of the performance of everyday life.

'Oscar Fingal O'Flahertie Wills Wilde,' wrote schoolmate Gordon Atkinson, 'as he signed himself in early days and filled two lines of paper doing it, was a personality even in 1874.'[2] Indeed, Wilde managed to create a personality at Oxford that was so memorable that, over twenty years later, the image of Wilde the outrageous aesthete superseded his work as a writer and the changes he made to his public persona. Years after Wilde's death, his son Vyvyan Holland included as an appendix in his autobiography a reminiscence by Wilde's Oxford friend William Ward, who wrote,

> One can see now, reading his character by the light of his later life, the beginnings of those tendencies which grew to his destruction. There was the love of pose, the desire for self-realization, the egotism, but they seemed foibles rather than faults.[3]

There is a great deal of convenient hindsight on Ward's part, but such was the potency of Wilde's aesthete persona at Oxford that it later served as the Wildean 'text' from which a cause for his disgrace could be found.

---

1 Richard Ellmann, *Oscar Wilde* (New York: Vintage, 1988), 9.

2 Gordon Atkinson, 'Oscar Wilde at Oxford,' *Cornhill Magazine* 66 (1929), 559.

3 W.W. Ward, 'Oscar Wilde: An Oxford Reminiscence,' in *Oscar Wilde: Interviews and Recollections* vol. 1, ed. E.H. Mikhail, 12–15 (London: Macmillan, 1979), 12. Originally published as an appendix to Vyvyan Holland, *Son of Oscar Wilde* (London: Rupert Hart-Davis, 1954).

At the time, however, Wilde impressed most of his classmates and dons as being a textbook representation of the aesthetic craze that had overtaken some university students in the 1870s. Francis Gribble, another Oxford friend, wrote that Wilde

> understood, as the pre-Raphaelites whom he succeeded had not understood it, the great art of posing – the art of challenging attention, not for what he had done but for what he was. He was the first to expound the art of life as the art of 'existing beautifully.'[4]

The art of Wilde's pose was that it was an act of the performance of everyday life, an act of Richard Schechner's concept of 'environmental theatre' – in this case, revisioning one's surroundings as a makeshift theatre and thereby reinscribing one's behaviour as a performance. For Schechner, 'the fundamental logic of environmental theatre is not the logic of the story but the logic of story-telling.'[5] As indicated by its gerundial form, 'story-telling' is a process, not a finished product. Schechner explains: 'The task of environmental theatre is to make process part of each performance. For the performer most of his daily work is process.'[6] The purpose of this process, according to Schechner, is discovery – a way to come upon truths and meanings not apparent in traditionally scripted and directed performances and a way to highlight the effect the process itself has on the discovery. A century prior to Schechner's own work with environmental theatre in New York, Wilde was conducting similar work with the ideas he was being exposed to at Oxford. As we shall see, his aesthetic poses and his belief in the art of beautiful living comes directly, sometimes in earnest and sometimes in irony, from his readings and participation in Oxford's in-

---

4 Francis Gribble, 'Oscar Wilde the Aesthete,' in *Oscar Wilde: Interviews and Recollections*, vol. 1, ed. E.H. Mikhail, 23–26 (London: Macmillan, 1979), 24.

5 Schechner, *Environmental Theater*, 83.

6 Ibid., 131.

tellectual life. Since the environment of everyday life is not scripted and therefore always carries with it a degree of unpredictability, process, not end product, is also the point of Wilde's performance. When Gribble writes that Wilde's talent was to call attention to who he was, he is the audience participating in Wilde's process – sometimes bemused or a little resistant, but one that witnesses Wilde's performance and makes an attempt to interpret it.

As can be imagined, however, not all the reactions to Wilde's performances were adulatory. Athletes in particular seemed to have scorned Wilde even though, by one student's account, Wilde was an excellent rower and was able to hold his own in a fistfight.[7] Gribble remembers students destroying Wilde's rooms after Wilde requested that the school's *Punch* subscription be cancelled (foreshadowing the cantankerous relations between the magazine and Wilde in the years to come).[8] And one anecdote, which may or may not be apocryphal, recounts how a group of athletes dragged Wilde to the top of a hill. After they released him, Wilde stood up and remarked, 'The view from this hill is really very charming.'[9]

Another anecdote about Wilde's strange but memorable behaviour takes place during his writing of the Divinations examination. Wilde had arrived at the examination late, excusing himself by saying, 'I have no experience at these pass examinations.' Offended that Wilde seemed to be insulting the rigor of his course, the examiner told Wilde to copy out the twenty-seventh chapter of Acts. After a short time, the examiner relented, but was startled to see Wilde continuing his work. When the examiner asked Wilde if he had not heard the order to stop writing, Wilde replied,

> Oh, yes, I heard you, but I was so interested in what I was copying that I could not leave off. It was all about a man named Paul, who went on a

7 Ellmann, *Oscar Wilde*, 44.

8 Gribble, 'Oscar Wilde the Aesthete,' 24.

9 Ellmann, *Oscar Wilde*, 43–44.

voyage and was caught in a terrible storm, and I was afraid that he would be drowned; but do you know, Mr. Spooner, he was saved; and when I found that he was saved, I thought of coming to tell you.[10]

Besides Wilde's knack for defusing a tense situation with a memorable punchline, he also created for himself a visual style that was at once fashionable for its time and outlandish in the eyes of the more conservative students and dons. He wore tweed jackets with large checks, accessorized them with bright blue neckties and curly-brimmed hats, and had a habit of flipping his long hair off his face with a pronounced gesture.[11] Along with his posing as a dilettante, as Sir David Hunter-Blair remembers, his colourful visual style and often provocative behaviour earned Wilde the reputation of being the leading practicing aesthete at Oxford.[12]

The result of these antics was that even though Wilde, according to one student, never dressed nor acted as outlandishly as some of the more fervent aesthetes, his remarks, dress and overall behaviour led other students to talk about him incessantly, either with disdain or in admiration. 'Probably no undergraduate ever attracted more attention while still an undergraduate,' writes Francis Gribble, 'or left a more enduring trail of legend behind him when he went down. . . . His sayings were quoted and anecdotes of his strange doings were passed round.'[13]

I want to stress a connection between Wilde's outrageous behaviour and self-consciously fashionable appearance with the particular focus of his intellectual curiosity. The fragments and copied

10 Douglas Sladen, 'Oscar Wilde at the Divinity Exam,' in *Oscar Wilde: Interviews and Recollections*, vol. 1, ed. E.H. Mikhail, 21–22 (London: Macmillan, 1979), 22.

11 See Ellmann, *Oscar Wilde*, 38, and Atkinson, 'Oscar Wilde at Oxford,' 559.

12 Sir David Hunter-Blair, 'Oscar Wilde at Magdalen College, Oxford,' in *Oscar Wilde: Interviews and Recollections*, vol. 1, ed. E.H. Mikhail, 3–12 (London: Macmillan, 1979), 5.

13 Gribble, 'Oscar Wilde the Aesthete,' 24.

material he put in his Oxford Notebooks point to a larger preoccupation with the definition and roots of an individual's personality, a preoccupation shared by liberal Victorians, Paterian aesthetes, and disciples of the Hellenic movement. Linda Dowling links these three groups together under a larger homoerotic discourse which began covertly to take shape at mid-century Oxford, one which I would argue eventually transforms much of Wilde's theories of performance. She writes that Victorian liberalism's appropriation of Hellenism prompts Wilde 'to see in "Greek love" itself the promise of a Hellenic individuality and diversity with the most positive implications for Victorian civilization.'[14] Wilde, foremost a man of ideas, wanted to reconcile the aesthetic splendour of the visual arts and the sensual excitement of contemplating the eroticized male body with the various philosophical tenets he was reading at the time, hoping, as an eager undergraduate, to make his ideas universal. As he matures as a writer, we see him temper his attempt to create a totalizing theory. But to define a fairly nebulous aspect of an individual, one who is more subject to idiosyncrasies than to moral or natural laws, and to use that as the basis for his thinking marks the beginning of what Jonathan Dollimore calls Wilde's 'transgressive aesthetic' and 'anti-humanist stance'.[15]

For Wilde, focusing on personality as the locus of art also is rooted in contemporary concerns, particularly the mid-1870s' cultural anxiety about the increasing mechanization of industry and the growing speed of technology. In this so-called 'age of progress,' questions arose as to whether the individual should not be viewed in mechanical terms, as a unit whose purpose is to aid in the smooth function of the larger social entity. Sociologist Herbert Spencer describes society as a creature evolving from its Darwinian adapta-

14 Linda Dowling, *Hellenism and Homosexuality in Victorian Oxford* (Ithaca and London: Cornell University Press, 1994), 66.

15 Dollimore, *Sexual Dissidence*, 8.

tion to its surroundings. '[E]ach institution,' he writes, 'draws to itself units of the society and nutriment for them, and tends ever to multiply and ramify.'[16] In Spencer's evolutionary philosophy, the individual has importance only in so far as he or she represents an aspect of the greater social whole. The duty of the individual therefore is to cultivate him- or herself only to further society's progress.

Evolutionary ideas about the individual were buttressed by existing theories of determinism. Determinism and its offshoots, notably Jean-Baptiste Lamarck's theory of heredity, circumscribed the individual by maintaining that one's sense of self is nothing more than the result of generations of accumulated family traits.[17] To a determinist, the individual therefore is merely a reflection of a greater, shared family character. But Spencer's application of evolutionary theory to Victorian society and Lamarck's belief that every individual is born circumscribed by pre-existing family characteristics, although faithful to middle-class Victorian ideals of duty, bloodline, and family loyalty, sat uneasily with the more Romantic proclivities of Wilde, who saw in his own heritage and behaviour traits that would perpetually keep him at the margins of his classmates' social sphere.

At this point, Wilde turns to Hegel's idealism and most notably the Hegelian dialectic with one exception: the absence of a synthesizing conclusion. Dollimore notes that Wilde's subversion of binaries links him closely with postmodern, deconstructive readings,[18]

16 Herbert Spencer, *The Study of Sociology*, 1873 (New York: D. Appleton, 1896), 17.

17 See John A. Lester, Jr., *Journey Through Despair 1880–1914: Transformations in British Literary Culture* (Princeton: Princeton University Press, 1968). Lamarck's theory of heredity was adopted by Darwin and used in his theory of acquired characteristics. Lamarckianism, as it was called, is not to be confused with the neo-Lamarckianism of George Bernard Shaw, who saw the inheritance of acquired characteristics as the individual being potentially able to pass on newly-acquired traits to succeeding generations.

18 Dollimore, *Sexual Dissidence*, 64.

but, also, his interest in Hegel (one of the more frequent subjects in his Notebooks) points to an older and more Romantic ideal. Simply put, for Wilde, synthesis is the unattainable ideal, since he imbues Hegel's synthesis with almost Blakean apocalyptic notes. In one Notebook entry, Wilde copies out John Addington Symonds' contention in *Studies of the Greek Poets* that Blake is one of the continuants of the Greek spirit.[19] In another entry, the echoes of Blake are apparent in William Wallace's 'Prelogomena' to *The Logic of Hegel*, which Wilde copies:

> Hegel made God the object of his philosophy – God the Original Synthetic Unity from which the non-ego and the ego have issued by differentiation, and in which they return to unity. For the Ego and the non-ego are equally the results of a process – the difficulty of spanning the chasm in one made by men for themselves.[20]

Self and other, subject and object are both fragments of a divine whole and it is the *active* tension between thesis and antithesis then (as his later epigrams demonstrate) that marks the human experience. If one concedes aspects of the self as being constructed by external conditions, then one must also accept the consciously-developing individual and hold both of these perspectives at once, constantly negotiating between the two opposite viewpoints.

This is one area where Wilde's 'performances' engage with his readings, and he performs his own personality to subvert Spencer's and Lamarck's ideas, conforming to the behaviour of the upper-class Oxford students while distinguishing himself from them at the same time. Wilde was self-conscious about his poses from his first days at Oxford, when he rid himself of both his Irish accent and

---

19 Oscar Wilde, *Oscar Wilde's Oxford Notebooks: A Portrait of Mind in Making*, ed. and intro. Philip E. Smith II and Michael S. Helfand (New York: Oxford University Press, 1989), 138.

20 Ibid., 148.

his lisp.[21] He also parodied the role of the aesthete to the bewilderment of his classmates, such as the time when, according to his classmate Douglas Sladen,

> he banished all the decorations from his rooms, except a single blue vase of the true aesthetic type which contained a 'Patience' lily. He was discovered by the other undergraduates of Magdalen prostrated with grief before it because he never could live up to it.[22]

The changes Wilde made to his speech, dress and mannerisms were a way of using performance to refute the curtailing theories of Darwin, Spencer, and Lamarck; in addition, he demonstrated that his Irish heritage was something that, through his aesthetic performance, he could refashion into something new. Wilde came to Oxford as an older student, having previously attended Trinity University at Dublin and, despite his father's knighthood and mother's fame, was resolutely middle class in a cohort filled with the sons of aristocrats and even Queen Victoria's son Prince Leopold. Early on, performance became a way for Wilde to distinguish himself and command attention to a group of students would otherwise have been prone to ostracizing him. This method of reinscribing himself into the dominant culture carries with it the element of camp that has long been associated with Wilde and, in this context, camp is indeed a part of Wilde's theory of performance. As Moe Meyer, who conflates the terms 'camp' and 'queer', argues,

> What queer signals in an ontological challenge that displaces bourgeois notions of the Self as unique, abiding, and continuous while substituting in-

21 Ellmann, *Oscar Wilde*, 38.
22 Sladen, 'Oscar Wilde at the Divinity Exam,' 21.

stead a concept of the Self as performative, improvisational, discontinuous, and processually constituted by repetitive and stylized acts.[23]

It has been a staple of queer readings of Wilde to argue a point corresponding to the one Meyer makes (including Gary Schmidgall's assertion that homosexuality is at the core of Wilde's sense of himself),[24] reading Wilde as reinscribing heterosexual societal norms with a gay aesthetic. In this case, Wilde's camp or queer performance is actually not restricted to sexuality – addressing class and nation at times – even though it is at the same time inherently rooted in a gay aesthetic.

Intellectually, Wilde's ideas about art and his application of these ideas to performance begin with a tension between the humanistic individual and Victorian evolutionary theories. However, although he only once mentions Matthew Arnold and his Hellenist theories of art and criticism in his Oxford Notebooks, there is an undercurrent in his note-taking of arguing against much of Arnold's writings, particularly 'The Function of Criticism in the Present Time' which Wilde read while at Oxford. Arnold, the Chair of Poetry at Oxford from 1857 to 1867, was precisely the voice of critical authority that Wilde sought to define himself against. In 'The Function of Criticism in the Present Time,' published in 1865 as part of *Essays in Criticism*, Arnold argues that criticism needs to be revalued in order for it to approach creative art's higher form of expression. He claims that since creativity is born out of an atmosphere of high intellectual and spiritual quality, the critic's task is to disseminate the ideas that will raise the calibre of this atmosphere

---

23 Moe Meyer, 'Introduction: Reclaiming the Discourse of Camp,' in *The Politics and Poetics of Camp*, ed. Moe Meyer, 1–21 (London: Routledge, 1994), 2–3.

24 Gary Schmidgall, *The Stranger Wilde: Interpreting Oscar* (New York: Dutton, 1994), xiv.

for the artist.[25] To accomplish this task, the critic needs to concentrate on the idea behind the image or text, to analyze and categorize his own intellectual and emotional reactions, and to assume a disinterested stance in his explanation of ideas.

Arnold's approach is based on the classical structure of human psychology, where reason sits loftily above the lower affects of emotion and sensation. The turn towards aesthetic matters led by the Hellenist movement, the successes of the Pre-Raphaelite Brotherhood and the cult following for Walter Pater's writings resulted in a return to the Romantic inversion of this structure, one which privileges perception and sensation as the most immediate, and therefore the truest, human response to external phenomena. Perception was usually considered by classical scholars to be a primitive response; the individual was expected to overcome his perceptions as quickly as possibly by rationalizing them. Benjamin Jowett, in his 1871 work on Plato's dialogues, describes Plato's conception of knowledge as 'the comparison of sensations with one another [which] implies a principle which is *above* sensation, and which resides in the mind itself.'[26] The mind, according to Jowett's interpretation, is comprised of three levels: perception, opinion, and reason. Perception is the immediate response to an object, and opinion consists of an emotional response to it; both must cede to the rational response if true understanding is to take place.

The limits imposed by the classical structure of mind, however, does not allow for the modern artist, the one who, according to Charles Baudelaire, must 'distil the eternal from the transitory' using

---

25 Matthew Arnold, 'The Function of Criticism at the Present Time,' in *The Complete Prose Works of Matthew Arnold*, vol. 3: Lectures and Essays in Criticism, ed. R.H. Super, 258–85 (Ann Arbor: University of Michigan Press, 1960–1977).

26 Benjamin Jowett, 'Introduction to 'Theaetetus,'' in *The Dialogues of Plato*, vol. 4, 3rd ed., ed. Benjamin Jowett (London: Oxford University Press, 1892), 116. Emphasis mine.

his physical self as the still,[27] to create new forms of knowledge through new effects. If art's meaning relies on the effect it produces, then for Wilde the sensational response needs to be accounted for in a way other than as a preliminary step on the way towards rational understanding. Sensation needs to be reclaimed as an important aspect of the thought process. In his Notebook, Wilde copies Jowett's concession to the role of sensation: 'Sensation seems to us simple; it is really most complex: till the mind applies it forms it is a "[confused thing]."'[28] Within this seeming confusion is the tension between reason and opinion – when experiencing a sensation, does one respond to it emotionally or rationally? Which response is the truer one? Instead of sensation and opinion working towards the development of reason, might reason and opinion exist in order to transform sensation into the primary source of knowledge?

To explore this possibility, Wilde turns to Thomas Huxley's interpretation of David Hume's reworking of the classical structure. Hume's variation of the structure reduces the three stages of the mind to two: impressions, which include both sensation and reflection or emotional reaction, and ideas, or reason. In his study, Huxley asserts that sensation, opinion and reason are nothing more than different categories of *perceptions*, and that the mind is a collection of different perceptions united by certain relations and presumed to have an identity. 'Hence,' writes Huxley,

> every predication is the verbal equivalent of a belief; and, as every belief is either an immediate consciousness, a memory; or an expectation, and as every

27 Charles Baudelaire, 'The Painter of Modern Life,' in *The Painter of Modern Life and Other Essays*, ed. and trans. Jonathan Mayne, 1–40 (London: Phaidon, 1964), 12.

28 Wilde, *Oxford Notebooks*, 133.

> expectation is traceable to a memory, it follows that, in the long run, all propositions express either immediate states of consciousness, or memories.[29]

For Huxley, Hume's idea of perception serves to make explicit and immediate the knowledge already residing within the individual. Reason makes this consciousness or memory known to the individual; its purpose is to identify and categorize. Wilde, calling Hume the 'champion of Sensationalism,' writes that Hume 'saw that apart from Sensation matter and mind are equally illusions.'[30] Wilde uses Huxley's interpretation of Hume to refigure perception as a valid intellectual position, and a basis from which the personality can express itself.

'Those who object to Metaphysics,' writes Wilde in his Notebooks,

> often mean no more than this[:] that all of our knowledge must be expressed in terms of the means by which knowledge is acquired, that is in terms ultimately reducible to statements about our sensations[,] therefore strictly relative[.][31]

Wilde's interest in the immediate responses to phenomena led him in 1879 to the lectures of William Kingdon Clifford, an optician and philosopher who studies the role of the mind in the physical act of seeing.[32] The development of new camera technologies such as the stereoscope (with which one could view two images simultaneously) and the Zoetrope (a succession of pictures appearing at small intervals) played a large part in Clifford's preoccupation with perception, since their ability to create images with illusory depth and motion altered the assumption that the eye recorded images faith-

29 Thomas Huxley, *Hume* (London: Macmillan, 1902), 63, 116.

30 Wilde, *Oxford Notebooks*, 120.

31 Ibid., 136.

32 Smith and Helfand date Wilde's encounter with Clifford's writings to the 1879 publication of Clifford's *Lectures and Essays*.

fully and without distortion. With both depth and motion being artificially reproduced, Clifford began to look at the human eye and mind in mechanical terms, asking how these biological features approximate the technological apparatuses.

In his lectures entitled 'The Philosophy of the Pure Sciences,' Clifford argues that the act of seeing is nothing more than the biological effects external data have on the eye and optic nerve.[33] The actual act of perception, or of making sense of the external data, requires the brain to imaginatively reconstruct the data. As Clifford remarks,

> The complete sensation which I have of a human head when I look at one is not merely something which I do not see now, but something which I never could see by any possibility. I have the sensation of a solid object, and not of a series of pictures of a solid object. Although that sensation may be really constructed out of a countless number of possible pictures, yet it is not like any of them. I imagine to myself, and seem to see the other side of things, not as it would look if viewed from beyond them, but as it would look if viewed from here. I seem to see the back of your head, not as it would look if I got behind you, but as if I saw it through your face from the spot where I am standing; and that, you know, is impossible.[34]

Perception, according to Clifford, is an act in which the mind superimposes an already-created coherent image on a series of fragmented visual stimuli. This image is drawn from the memory of having perceived similar data, or from the knowledge of commonly-agreed-upon laws, such as those of physics or geometry.[35] Both the law of heredity established by Lamarck and Spencer's collective race

---

33 William Kingdon Clifford, 'The Philosophy of the Pure Sciences,' in *Lectures and Essays*, vol. 1, ed. Leslie Stephen and Frederick Pollock, 254–340. (London: Macmillan, 1879), 255–256. First presented as a series of lectures at the Royal Institution in March 1873.

34 Ibid., 256–257.

35 Ibid., 260.

theory find their way into Clifford's optical theory through his assertion that commonly-inherited laws and ideas allow for human beings to share common perceptions of objects – that is, if there is a tree, our eyes will all register it as a tree and we will all see the same tree. Yet, although Clifford acknowledges the presence of a 'collective race memory,' to quote his reference to Spencer, his view of perception holds that no two people will see exactly the same object. Each person's individual experience acts in conjunction with commonly-accepted laws to form perception, but each person's experiences are formed out of the person's particular sense of self.

Drawing on analogies between human perception and new camera technologies, Clifford stresses that the object one sees is actually a *representation* of the thing itself, since one never has direct perceptual access to the thing as it really *is*.[36] Therefore each object's 'character' (the properties and qualities which make up the object) relies in part on the viewer's 'character,' since the viewer's sense of self motivates the perceptual choices he makes in reconstructing the object.[37] For Clifford, then, the self is the foundation for meaning and that, by cultivating the self, one can influence, within the limits set forth by society, the making of meaning. 'I shall conclude by analogy,' Clifford writes,

> that this world which I directly perceive is not really outside of me; that the things which are apparently made known to me by my perceptions are really themselves only groups of my perceptions; that the universe which I perceive is made up of my feelings; that in fact it is really *me*. And – by analogy also – I shall conclude that there *is* something besides this, different from it; the changes in which correspond in a certain way to the changes in my

36 The distinction between a thing and its representation relates to Schopenhauer's assertion that individuals understand a thing's meaning through their perception of it.

37 Clifford, 'The Philosophy of the Pure Sciences,' 272.

universe. Is it then possible for me to know which that is? or is there nothing at all except my feelings?[38]

According to Clifford's analogy, emotions exist in each individual as a network, forming links to external objects or people in order to connect to the individual's sense of self. All perceptions literally form along a current, transmitting the feelings of the other to the self where they are reprocessed according to the self's consciousness and then sent back out again.[39]

Wilde adapts Clifford's ideas about perception to imply that an individual's persona exists as a series of charges, brief images which flow in succession from self to other and are reconstructed in the other's mind by the use of his or her own consciousness, which he sees as the modern incarnation of the Platonic Absolute Idea. Consciousness, as a substitute for the Absolute Idea, is

> the one power which is able to weld together the isolated fragments into a true synthetic unity . . . and it does so by transporting them into a higher sphere – the sphere of pure thought – where matter and form, mind and nature, the Ego and the non-ego coincide.[40]

Therefore the more striking the image, the more likely it is to form a memory in the other's mind. For Wilde, Clifford's theory of perception, by discussing the idea of a self created out of a series of lived experiences which is able to influence the physical apprehension of objects, offers a humanist alternative to the concept of the mechanized individual.

In the spirit of uniting seemingly opposite patterns of thought, Wilde's study of Clifford's scientific philosophy and Hume's em-

---

38 Ibid., 286.

39 Ibid., 290. Clifford cites John Stuart Mill as the originator of the theory of emotions as cables.

40 Wilde, *Oxford Notebooks*, 128. Here Wilde is summarizing a section of William Wallace's 'Prolegomena.'

pirical philosophy leads him to apply these ideas to the field of art via both Walter Pater's works and the Hellenic revival of Greek art. Quoting Pater's essay on Winckelmann in *Studies in the History of the Renaissance*, Wilde writes in his Notebooks, 'Art then may be regarded as the natural expression of the spirit of man projecting itself in the forms of beauty most characteristic of its nature.'[41] A large part of the Notebooks involve Wilde trying to construct a perceptual, aesthetic history of the classical age which can act as a historical and intellectual foundation for his ideas about performance. The phrases Wilde copies emphasize the ancient Greeks conceiving of ideas in the form of images and explaining things in terms of the senses. Quoting John Addington Symonds, Wilde writes in his Notebooks that the Greeks 'always sought to externalise, to realise, to remain within corporeal limits' and Greek art 'translates into marble the humanised aspects of the external world.'[42] Characters in Greek drama, for instance, bore a symbol of their internal life upon their bodies, like Oedipus' and Teiresias' blindness. Artistic possibilities for the ancient Greeks were restricted only by the limitations of the body, and Wilde using his own dressed body as a medium for personality is a conscious evocation of this idea.

If Greek art (and here Wilde is using Arnold's assumptions about Greek art in *Culture and Anarchy*) is imagistic, externalized, and present only on its surface, modern art is by contrast abstract and emotional.[43] Continuing his quoting of Symonds, he writes in the Notebooks,

> Modern art appeals directly to the emotions, aims at reaching the spiritual reality of things, cares more for feelings than for form – Greek art remains

41 Ibid., 140.

42 Ibid., 139. This quote is taken from John Addington Symonds, *Studies of the Greek Poets*, II.

43 Baudelaire discusses the double nature of beauty as being both surface and interior in 'The Painter of Modern Life.'

on the surface and translates into marble the humanized aspects of the ex ternal world.[44]

Modern art's aim is spiritual truth rather than pictorial representation. Building 'a bridge between Greek and modern life' is one of his recurring preoccupations in the Notebooks.[45] The attempt to synthesize Greek and modern art becomes one of the fundamental concepts underlying his ideas about performance and persona: if he is putting forth the concept of living one's life as a work of art, then it is a Greek work of art, with a great deal of attention paid to form, but it is also a modern work of art in its attention to the simultaneous surface beauty and interior spirit. 'Only in art,' Julia Prewitt Brown notes in her discussion of Wilde's aesthetics, 'wherein spirit is embodied in the sensuous, do the ideal and empirical realms realize themselves and become "true."'[46] Art (whether a painting or poem or a cultivated personality) is the plastic expression of an individual's sense of self and represents the same relationship between surface and interior.

Wide prefigures Martin Heidegger's later assertion that

> [t]he artist is the origin of the work. The work is the origin of the artist. Neither is without the other. Nevertheless, neither is the sole support of the other. In themselves and in their interrelations artist and work *are* each of them by virtue of a third thing which is prior to both, namely that which also gives artist and work of art their names – art.[47]

---

44 Wilde, *Oxford Notebooks*, 139.

45 Ibid., 140. The quote is taken from Pater's 'Winckelmann' who in turn attributes it to Hegel's *Aesthetik*.

46 Julia Prewitt Brown, *Cosmopolitan Criticism: Oscar Wilde's Philosophy of Art* (Charlottesville, VA, and London: University Press of Virginia, 1997), xv.

47 Martin Heidegger, *Poetry, Language, Thought*, trans. and intro. Albert Hofstadter (New York: Harper Collins, 1971), 17.

If Clifford's theory of perception holds that emotions structure the way one sees all objects, then in attempting to synthesize surface and interior, Wilde holds that each individual channels his or her emotions from the externalized self-image to the internalized spirit, or consciousness, and back again. Thus the persona one projects influences one's sense of self as much as one's internal life shapes one's persona. This is in a sense proto-phenomenology (although not necessarily Heidegger's), in that anything created by an artist bears the trace of his or her persona and interpreting a work successfully will result in a spiritual communion with its creator.

Perhaps the strongest influence on Wilde's developing performance theory is Walter Pater, not least because of Pater's challenges to the same evolutionary school against which Wilde develops his ideas. Pater's *Studies in the History of the Renaissance*, first published in 1873, which Wilde later called 'that book which has had such a strange influence over my life,'[48] represents a break from some of the prevalent theoretical currents of the mid-Victorian period. His portraits of Renaissance figures and incitements to live the aesthetic life reconfigure the ideas of Spencer, Ruskin and Arnold into a world view which reasserts the individual as the locus of interpretation.[49]

In the mid-nineteenth century, British empirical philosophy and the nascent field of sociology had both begun to revisit the role of the individual in an age of industrial and national advances. The acknowledgement that the Victorians were part of a great age of 'progress' also uncovered an increasingly vexed relationship be-

48 Oscar Wilde, *De Profundis*, in *The Complete Letters of Oscar Wilde*, ed. Merlin Holland and Rupert Hart-Davis, 683–780 (New York: Henry Holt, 2000), 735.

49 See Steven Marcus, 'Conceptions of the Self in an Age of Progress,' in *Progress and Its Discontents*, ed. Gabriel A. Almond, Marvin Chodorow and Roy Harvey Pearce, 431–48 (Berkeley: University of Califonia Press, 1982); and Regenia Gagnier, 'The Law of Progress and the Ironies of Individualism in the Nineteenth Century,' *New Literary History* 31, no. 2 (2000), 315–36.

tween the individual and society. The question most often implied was this: in an age when evolution is seen as the progress of a species, imperialism as the progress of a nation, and industrialization as the progress of the middle class, is there room for a more humanist, less mechanized notion of the individual? And, as Jeffrey Wallen points out in his discussion of Pater, this re-centering of the individual in relationship to aesthetics runs the risk of 'narcissistic criticism': 'This constant recourse to figures of the self in Pater's writing risks the possibility of yielding the image of Pater's own "self" in the place of a vision of the artwork or the artist.'[50] The positivist approach to progress corresponds nicely to the Victorian reverence for duty, putting the individual in service to the greater social or national whole and Pater's aesthetic, by stressing the importance of cultivating different sensations and experiences in order to heighten one's aesthetic sensitivity, runs determinedly counter to this ideology, something which Wilde recognized and exploited in his writings.

The ideology of duty, of service to a greater social or national entity, is present in both Spencer and Arnold's works. Spencer's belief that each individual is a synecdoche of society argues for a collective individuality, each person retaining a ghost image, as it were, of the evolution of his society.[51] In 'The Function of Criticism in the Present Time,' Arnold uses the dichotomy between self and society to encourage the individual to do his duty and apply his critical perceptions in service to England. Moreover, Arnold's insistence that criticism should 'see the object as it really is' posits a

---

50 Jeffrey Wallen, 'Reflection and Self-Reflection: Narcissistic or Aesthetic Criticism?,' *Texas Studies in Literature and Language* 34, no. 3 (1992), 302.

51 Spencer, *The Study of Sociology*, 17. Lamarck's theory that each individual is an aggregate of his ancestors' characteristics is yet another permutation of the individual as a unit of a greater whole. For a discussion of neo-Lamarckian theory and its implications on the late Victorians, see Lester, *Journey Through Despair*, 43.

truth that exists irrespective of subjective interpretation.[52]

As a challenge to Arnold's criticism, *The Renaissance* reasserts the individual critic as the most vital interpretive source for a work of art. Pater insists that the individual's own artistry is the ideal medium for interpretation and that this artistry is also responsible for the ethos or spirit of an age.[53] But, as Wallen notes, Pater uses his argument that the Renaissance exists because of its artists in order to put forth a critical strategy which has the self's own impressions and aesthetic sensibility determine the nature and importance of art:

> The efficacy of the portrait, as a form for exploring all that the artwork expresses, rests on the assumption that the 'self' offers an accessibility and also a unity of thought and feeling that the work does not.[54]

More than just a narcissistic glorification of the self, however, Pater's use of portraiture in *The Renaissance* argues for an exchange of personae, an idea that Wilde develops later in his critical essays. The work of art can be understood best through the impressions of the critic. Further study into the work of art reveals a portrait of the artist; in true artistic terms, the artist is an image constructed out of the critic's encounter with the art. The critic understands art through his interpretation of the artwork itself and the artist as a work of art, both of which are affected by the critic's own self-cultivation. For example, Pater's meditation on La Gioconda implicitly imposes traces of Leonardo's personality onto the painting – not the actual Leonardo, but the one constructed in the critic's mind out of an engagement with his work. By looking at the painting, one sees this image of Leonardo; by loving the painting, one absorbs Leonardo's genius – not merely his artistic ability, but the personality that gives form to his talent. By absorbing his genius, one's own capacity for

52 Matthew Arnold, 'The Function of Criticism at the Present Time,' 258.

53 Pater, *The Renaissance*, xxi.

54 Wallen, 'Reflection and Self-Reflection,' 302.

artistry (in this case, the art of criticism) evolves. It is an aesthetic based on the self but on a self constantly developing from its exposure to others.

Indeed, Pater's description of La Gioconda encapsulates the exchange of personae that figures so heavily in his work. In meditating upon the painting's creation, he remarks,

> From childhood we see the image defining itself on the fabric of [Leonardo's] dreams; and but for express historical testimony, we might fancy that this was but his ideal lady, embodied and beheld at last. What was the relationship of a living Florentine to this creature of his thought? By what strange affinities had the dream and the person grown up thus apart, and yet so closely together? Present from the first incorporeally in Leonardo's brain, dimly traced in the designs of Verrochio, she is found present at last in *Il Giocondo*'s house.[55]

Pater isolates the interplay between Leonardo's desire, memory, and unconscious, as well as the relationship between the artist and his model's persona, which results in the portrait. Thus the persona of La Gioconda acts as a mediation between the critic's persona and the artwork, encouraging the critic to develop his artistry out of this relationship. In Pater's case, the development takes the form of lush and ornate writing, intending to echo textually the art which it discusses. 'The presence that rose thus so strangely beside the waters,' he writes in his famous description of La Gioconda, 'is expressive of what in the ways of a thousand years men had come to desire.'[56] Unlike Arnold's work of art, seeing this object as it really is involves a uniting of critic, artwork, and artist, where different selves meet to form an impression of the work that can also be integrated into an overall way of living.

55 Pater, *The Renaissance*, 97–98.

56 Ibid., 98.

The emphasis Pater puts on the self in his criticism complicates conventional ideas about the self as either unified or stable. Linda Dowling notes that Pater 'wished to show that even the self, a category that was less a category than the very precondition *for* experience, was subject to vicissitudes of change.'[57] Being subject to change becomes the precursor to Wilde's notion of the self as inherently fragmented and divided against itself, in a dialectical relationship with both itself and the outside world. More importantly, it is also the precursor to Wilde's notion of the self as divided into actor and play, or text which is performed.

What becomes important to Wilde is the argument that the synthesizing of one's aesthetic responses into a performance – whether a virtuoso written piece, a painting, a stage performance, or a memorable mode of behaviour – becomes an especially powerful critical tool because it is art in itself. In order to achieve this effect, the self is always in the process of being reshaped by the different artistic influences it encounters. A decade after he left Oxford, Wilde wrote a review of Pater's *Appreciations* for the *Speaker*, which included the following passage:

> To know anything about oneself, one must know all about others. There must be no mood with which one cannot sympathise, no dead mode of life that one cannot make alive. The legacies of heredity may make us alter our views of moral responsibility, but they cannot but intensify our sense of the value of Criticism; for the true critic is he who bears within himself the dreams and ideas and feelings of myriad generations, and to whom no form of thought is alien, no emotional impulse obscure.[58]

57 Linda Dowling, 'Walter Pater and the Matter of the Self,' in *Die Modernisierung des Ich: Studien zur Subjecktkinstitution in der Ver- und Frühmoderne*, ed. Manfred Pfister, 64–73 (Passau: Wissenschaftsverlag Richard Rothe, 1989), 69.

58 Oscar Wilde, 'Mr. Pater's Last Volume,' in *The Artist as Critic: Critical Writings of Oscar Wilde*, ed. Richard Ellmann, 229–234 (Chicago: University of Chicago Press, 1969), 230.

The self's performance is therefore not just solipsism on display; it incorporates the influences of others' performances and reshapes them into something novel enough to attract the attention of someone else, who will presumably undergo the same process. Pater, Lamarckian theory, and the power of sensation all meld into Wilde's ideas about criticism here, which are in this context also his ideas about performance.

It might be fitting to end the discussion of Pater and his influence on Wilde where both of these writers begin, with a consideration of the beautiful. Beauty, for Pater, is as complex a state as the self designed to appreciate it. It is the locus for sensation, that initial response that actually structures all other responses. According to Pater in 'The School of Giorgione,' beauty manifests itself in objects as a 'primary aspect,'[59] one single unique quality which each work of art expresses:

> This *drawing*, then – the arabesque traced in the air by Tintoret's flying figures, by Titian's forest branches' this colouring – the magic conditions of light and hue in the atmosphere of Titian's *Lace-girl*, or Rubens's *Descent from the Cross*: – these essential pictorial qualities must first of all delight the sense, delight it as directly and sensuously as a fragment of Venetian glass; and through this delight alone become the vehicle of whatever poetry or science may lie beyond them in the intention of the composer.[60]

The primary aspect is the first thing perceived and imparts its meaning through sensation, especially through delight.

Beauty therefore comes into existence by way of the relationship between the individual and the work of art. To have beauty achieve this goal, Pater adopts a system where beauty is both the

59 Walter Pater, 'The School of Giorgione,' *Fortnightly Review* 22 (1877), 526–528, rpt. in *The Renaissance*, 104.

60 Ibid.

subjective response to art and the essential unity from which different forms of art emerge. He writes in *The Renaissance*:

> To define beauty, not in the most abstract, but in the most concrete terms possible, not to find a universal formula for it, but the formula which expresses most adequately this or that special manifestation of it, is the aim of the true student of aesthetics.[61]

Both beauty and art occupy interdependent, somewhat paradoxical roles in Pater's writing: beauty is an aspect of art in some places, art is an aspect of beauty in others. He describes art as being a union of matter and form, with form being the dominant aspect.[62] Moreover, art is constantly engaged in a struggle against interpretation and against the critic who insists on placing it in a tidy category. For Pater, the ideal state of art

> often appears to depend, in part, on a certain suppression or vagueness of mere subject, so that the meaning reaches us through ways not distinctly traceable by the understanding.[63]

Art is always striving to be independent of the intellect, to be a matter of pure perception.[64] The intellect, after all, is both the constructor and the product of a circumscribed symbolic order. Art's power, on the contrary, lies in its ability to transcend its own rules of matter and form and produce one single, unified effect on the individual. This single effect, though, is an illusion – it conceals the fragmentary, multifaceted nature of all art. The critic's responsibility, according to both Pater and Wilde, is not merely to lay bare the different fragments, but to explore each of them as a single artistic effect as well, in a process of potentially infinite regression.

61 Pater, *The Renaissance*, vii.

62 Pater, 'The School of Giorgione,' 106.

63 Ibid., 108.

64 Ibid.

Arnold's dictum of truth in an object then does not fit with this more Romanticized view of art; art's truth is present in Pater's criticism, but it is an impressionistic, subjective truth rather than an objective one.

Where Wilde departs from Pater is in the construction of a consciously theatrical self. Pater disdains overt theatricality; he uses it as a descriptor of a 'worn-out society, theatrical in its life, theatrical in its art, theatrical even in its devotion.'[65] For Pater, theatricality is artifice, 'the presence of mimes and flute players,' which reduces a great work of art to 'mere portraiture' or a great work of criticism to a series of shallow observations.[66] Wilde, on the other hand, is fascinated with the relationship between the plastic and performing arts. One entry from his Notebook, taken again from Symonds, is a meditation on the effect of theatre on the history of ideas:

> [C]ompare Aristophanes particularily [*sic*] for this peculiar sensible symbolism – the real <u>scales</u> in which Æschylus and Euripides are weighed, the <u>mortar</u> in which War and havoc bray up the states of Greece, are like [force] and [might] of the Prometheus, and entirely in accordance with the Greek attitude . . .
>
> How much of this is due to the fact that Greek Literature was not meant to be <u>read</u> – but to be recited.[67]

Moreover, Wilde's theatrical behaviour at Oxford showed him that his own persona could be cultivated as a work of art. When Wilde dressed in aesthetic clothing or used his storytelling ability to mesmerize his fellow students, he recognized that performance, even in the absence of a stage or of the expectation of theatre, can still inspire an aesthetic response. Oxford was the place where he

---

65 Pater, *The Renaissance*, 81.

66 Ibid., 98.

67 Wilde, *Oxford Notebooks*, 138. The first passage is a quote from Symonds's *Studies of the Greek Poets*. The second passage is Wilde's commentary.

began to understand the relationship between performance and the critical spirit he identified in his study of the Ancient Greeks. As he explored the ramifications of performance in his writings, he also understood that by using his own self to demonstrate the theories he was working with, he could explore their implications in a way the written word was ill-equipped to do.

Chapter Two
Celebrity, Caricatures and Public Performances in the 1880s

While still a student at Oxford, Wilde once flippantly stated, 'I find it harder and harder every day to live up to my blue china.' The remark was typical of Wilde's delight in annoying the Philistines, and not surprisingly the remark horrified Dean Burgon of St. Mary's College who, in a vitriolic Sunday sermon, attacked it and the new form of 'heathenism' it represented.[1] The *Oxford and Cambridge Undergraduate's Journal* picked up the story and in an 1879 article used both Wilde and his blue-china remark as examples of the contemporary Aesthetic Movement. The remark gained widespread attention when *Punch* used it satirically in 1880, a year after Wilde had left Oxford.[2] Throughout the 1880s *Punch*'s George du Maurier used Wilde as the model for the aesthete in his caricatures and satirical captions. Long-haired and languorous, lost in contemplation over a lily or a sunflower and speaking in cryptic aphorisms about beauty, *Punch*'s Oscuro Wildegoose, Ossian Wilderness and Drawit Milde, among other epithets, became the defining caricatures of the aesthete for du Maurier and eventually for other magazine artists. Although Wilde changed his dress and witticisms a number of times after leaving Oxford, these early caricatures were the genesis of a spate of satirical drawings and articles and became the foundation of Wilde's image as an aesthete in the 1880s.

---

1 Ellmann, *Oscar Wilde*. 45.

2 Ibid.

Wilde's minor celebrity status in the 1880s proved to be both a blessing and a curse. To an extent, Wilde cultivated the media attention, no matter how derisive, and Regenia Gagnier argues that 1880s culture created a milieu that encouraged a celebrity borne out of image and caricature: 'in this beginning of the age of modern advertising, the press was easily accessible for self-advertisement; the upper classes [...] were enthusiastic for all kinds of fads and amusements.'[3] Fresh out of university, Wilde inserted himself into popular culture by way of outlandish dress and epigrams, much in the same way he made himself known at Oxford. But the 1880s also was the period where Wilde was himself experimenting with different performances which at their most elementary levels reflected the massive changes he underwent in both his personal and his professional life: in this decade, he gave a series of lectures in the United States and Canada as the representation of England's Aesthetic Movement, he married Constance Lloyd and fathered two sons, he worked as a journalist and reviewer in order to support his family and later became editor of *The Woman's World*, he wrote two plays and saw both of them fail to capture an audience, and, most famously, he had his first homosexual love affair. Wilde went from knee breeches to more sedate dress and experimented more with public performance than with developing his theory in his writing (although he did not neglect his intellectual work). All of this performative work culminates in his writings of the very late 1880s into the 1890s and his status as a public figure contributes to this work.

But the press, as Wilde discovered, was much like the devil he described in his fairy tale 'The Fisherman and His Soul' – namely the one who watches him dance knowing that its price will be exacted. As Laurel Brake has argued, late-Victorian periodicals competed in a crowded marketplace by constituting a particular 'identity,' which she claims is constructed out of the relationship between the edi-

3 Gagnier, *Idylls of the Marketplace*, 14.

torial board, the writers, and the periodical's readership.[4] Despite Wilde's changing persona and despite some of the more thoughtful essays he wrote during this period such as 'The English Renaissance of Art' and his editorials in the early issues of *The Woman's World*, the silly aesthete languishing in knee breeches remained his best-known public image.

Thus the concept of persona and performance of the self becomes a question of agency for Wilde, and takes a more immediate turn than when he mused about it at Oxford. Specifically, Wilde notes that there is a definite connection between the public self and the sense of one's own subjectivity, and whoever controls a person's public self controls a person's identity. Wilde is not oblivious to the effect of culture and society on the development of an individual's identity – his readings of Spencer, Lamarck and Pater attest to his awareness of social conditioning – but he comes to see identity as located in the struggle for agency over one's public persona. Returning to Hegel, he sees the public persona as a dialectic between self-realization and conditioned response; it is not until his critical essays that he looks towards synthesizing these oppositions. Rather than didactically writing about this struggle, Wilde instead performs it, both publicly and textually in his early works, sometimes proactively and sometimes in reaction to nationalist and racist cartoons and articles in the press.

The press' cartoons of Wilde can be divided into two groups: the relatively benign ridicule of Wilde as a silly but harmless aesthete which describes the British press' attitude towards him before his tour of America, and the more sinister depictions of him in the cartoons that are created during and after the tour. The American press was largely responsible for this shift in the caricatures. Whereas the English newspapers dismissed Wilde as more or less a

4 Laurel Brake, *Subjugated Knowledges: Journalism, Gender and Literature in the Nineteenth Century* (New York: New York University Press, 1994), 11.

novelty act in London society, the American press, faced with a sensibility in Wilde's lectures at odds with the idealized concept of the American man and appalled by the popularity of his lectures, presented Wilde in considerably more malignant terms. The caricatures of Wilde prior to his tour depict him as an effete proselytizer whose threat lies in leading English men and women into unproductive artistic reveries. But the caricatures of Wilde during his tour transform Wilde into a sexual predator, one who uses aesthetic words to seduce innocent youth of both genders into artistic and sensual dissolution.

Early caricatures of Wilde have him dressed stylishly but relatively conservatively compared to what he purportedly wore at Oxford. This figure is distinguishable from the ordinary Victorian gentleman in body language rather than dress. An 1880 caricature by du Maurier entitled 'Maudle on the Choice of a Profession' shows the Wilde figure slouching almost seductively towards the proper Mrs. Brown. The caption reads:

> *Maudle.* How *consummately* lovely your Son is, Mrs. Brown!
>
> *Mrs. Brown (a Philistine from the country). What!* He's a *nice, manly* Boy, if you mean *that*, Mr. Maudle. He has just left School, you know, and wishes to be an Artist.
>
> *Maudle. Why* should he be an Artist?
>
> *Mrs. Brown.* Well, he must be *something*!
>
> *Maudle.* Why should he *Be* anything? Why not let him remain for ever content to *Exist Beautifully?*
>
> *[Mrs. Brown determines that at all events her Son shall not study Art under Maudle.*[5]

5 George du Maurier, 'Maudle on the Choice of a Profession.' *Punch*, 30. October 1880.

Here it is important to note Alan Sinfield's argument that until Wilde's trials in 1895, effeminacy was not a culturally-recognized sign of homosexuality but rather a sign of a decadent and soft aristocracy.[6] Wilde's aestheticism in du Maurier's caricature is linked to the latter type of effeminacy which poses a threat to English youth, not only because of the attention paid to style and dress, but because it reverses the relationship between the genders and work. Here, the young boy is supposedly the passive object of beauty and of Maudle's aesthetic gaze and, like a pretty girl at the time, his purpose in life should be the cultivation of his beauty. By exaggerating aesthetic proclamations and connecting them specifically to the decadent slouch of Maudle, du Maurier paints Wilde as a figure of ridicule. He can pose no threat to British manliness, in other words, because he is not quite a man himself.

The image of Wilde as harmlessly effeminate is repeated in a cartoon entitled 'Aesthetics v. Athletics' (Figure 1) which shows the aesthete caught in a stampede of racing schoolboys. The muscular Christianity of these future soldiers of the Empire is indeed about to trample the useless aesthete into the ground. Attempting to keep his balance, the Wilde figure hilariously laments, 'This is indeed a form of death, and entirely incompatible with any belief in the immortality of the soul.'

Throughout the early 1880s Wilde was always associated with women, whether in caricatures of his posture or topics of discussion or by portraying him surrounded by a female audience. For instance, W.P. Frith's 1881 painting *A Private View at the Royal Academy* shows Wilde lecturing to a small group of beautifully-dressed women while the more sombrely-dressed men look sceptically at him from a distance. The implication in the painting is that the women are listening to Wilde (who is dressed more colourfully than the other male

6 Alan Sinfield, *The Wilde Century: Effeminacy, Oscar Wilde and the Queer Moment* (New York: Columbia University Press, 1994), 71.

Figure 1. 'Aesthetics v. Athletics.' 1881. Oscar Wilde and His Literary Circle. William Andrews Clark Memorial Library, University of California, Los Angeles.

figures in the painting) speak about art and his words are influencing the way they perceive the paintings. Thus while the caricatures see the Wilde figure as ineffective at converting the male population to aestheticism, Frith's painting suggests a strong affinity between Wilde and women. It economically trivializes Wilde's aesthetics by feminizing it, and the inclusion of several children who seem most interested in Wilde further trivializes him as well.

At this point, Wilde's aestheticism leaned more towards a sort of androgynous performance, a way of playing gender roles against each other. Joseph Bristow writes, 'By 1889, the effeminate man could be seen to embody an androgynous ideal and yet instantly betray it by seeming to be womanly.'[7] The 'seeming' is telling here, since the perspective would be biased towards traditional expressions of masculinity. Wilde helps to create the effeminate man in the 1880s by conflating aesthetic and gender performances (playing on the affinity between aesthetes and women portrayed by Frith in his painting) which in turn leads to a revival of the Regency and Baudelairean dandies in the 1890s. Gender becomes performance as *bricolage* or as intertext. As Philip Auslander notes, 'The performing body is always doubly encoded – it is defined by the codes of a particular performance but has always already been inscribed, in its material aspect, by social discourses.'[8] Depending on one's point of view, Wilde the aesthete is an effeminate man or a Romantic artist, a figure of great interest or great ridicule, a harmless diversion or a thinly-disguised lecher.

Wilde's 1882 lecture tour of the United States and Canada proved to be a turning point with respect to his celebrity status, the performance of his persona, and the way in which his persona was manipulated by the press. The tour was the idea of impressario

7 Joseph Bristow, *Effeminate England: Homoerotic Writing After 1895* (New York: Columbia University Press, 1995), 7.

8 Auslander, *From Acting to Performance*, 90.

Richard D'Oyly Carte who was producing a tour of Gilbert and Sullivan's operetta *Patience*. A lampoon of the Aesthetic Movement, *Patience* features a character, Reginald Bunthorne, who displays many of the qualities of the caricatures of Wilde. Although Bunthorne was a composite of several aesthetes, Whistler among them, and not just a satire of Wilde, D'Oyly Carte proposed to Wilde that he tour North America as the 'real' Bunthorne and deliver lectures on aesthetic matters.

One of the first stops Wilde made upon his arrival in New York in January 1882 was to famed photographer Napoleon Sarony's studio. The visit to Sarony was the idea of Wilde's tour manager, Colonel W.F. Morse, who thought that photographs of Wilde by Sarony (famous for his celebrity portraits, most notably those of Sarah Bernhardt) would help to promote the tour.[9] Sarony shot twenty-seven stills of Wilde in various kinds of arty costumes: knee breeches, fur coat, velvet cape. Because the photographs would not be ready for the first lecture, Wilde and Morse asked New York artist James Edward Kelly to sketch Wilde as he posed for the photographs.[10] The sketches were then published in New York newspapers to advertise Wilde's lecture. A page is devoted to some of these sketches in the 21 January 1882 issue of *Frank Leslie's Illustrated Newspaper* (Figure 2). Included among the sketches of the Sarony photographs is a drawing of Wilde lecturing. In a sketch of the Frith painting, Wilde is again speaking to a group of women while the male audience members stand on the side, out of Wilde's range of vision and presumably distanced from the things he had to say. Wilde and Morse also sold the sketches to advertisers and soon the image of Wilde posing in knee breeches and standing next to a sunflower was being used to sell various goods from cigars to ice cream (Figure 3).

9 Barbara Belford, *Oscar Wilde: A Certain Genius* (New York: Random House, 2000), 94.

10 Ibid., 95.

Figure 2. 'Oscar Wilde, the Apostle of Aestheticism. From a photograph by Sarony.' *Frank Leslie's Illustrated Newspaper*, Jan 21 1882. William Andrews Clark Memorial Library, Los Angeles, California.

This increased exposure of Wilde, however, was ill-timed: while he was touring America, Charles Guiteau, a disgruntled office-seeker, evangelist and former member of the socialist Oneida group, was on trial for the shooting of President Garfield. Guiteau's religious fervour and flamboyant personality, coupled with the sensationalism of his crime, earned him a considerable amount of notoriety, and his sermons from the dock were so charismatically delivered that he amassed a group of sympathizers.[11] Wilde, with his own flamboyant personality, aesthetic fervour, and the warm reception he was given by many of his audiences, reminded the conservative press sufficiently of Guiteau to represent yet another potential threat to the moral fabric of American society, his aesthetic pronouncements a sign of European degeneration, his effeminate demeanour as dangerous as a would-be presidential assassin. The caricatures of Wilde in the American newspapers were much more sinister than their British counterparts. For instance, the *Washington Post* printed a cartoon of an ape and of Wilde with the title 'Mr. Wild of Borneo' and the caption: 'How far is it from THIS [the Wild Man of Borneo] to THIS [Wilde the aesthete]?'[12] When Colonel Morse complained to the *Post* about the caricature, the editor cruelly replied, 'Nature never makes a mistake. [She] never puts the brains of a man of mental brawn and vigor into the cavity faced by such a physiognomy as that of Oscar Wilde's.'[13]

In American periodicals, Wilde became a sign for all sorts of racist and chauvinist attitudes, especially those that perceived black Americans and foreigners as a threat to the moral vigour of the nation. One caricature in *Harper's Weekly* shows a grotesque Wilde, his head elongated to resemble a mushroom cap, looming menacingly

11 Lloyd Lewis and Henry Justin Smith, *Oscar Wilde Discovers America [1882]* (New York: Benjamin Blom, 1967), 96.

12 Ibid.

13 Ibid., 100.

Figure 3. Advertisement based on Sarony photograph. Oscar Wilde and His Literary Circle. William Andrews Clark Memorial Library, University of California, Los Angeles.

over a group of feminine-looking sunflowers (Figure 4). The caricature is titled 'The British Fungus and the *Wild* American Sunflowers,' categorizing Wilde as one of those decadent effeminate foreigners and his threat to the 'natural' American way of life. The caricature is a parody of the pictures that have Wilde surrounded by rapt women; the expressions of the sunflowers range from bewilderment to disdain. Belabouring the point, the caricature includes a 'quote' from Wilde, in actuality the famous quote from Keats' 'Ode on a Grecian Urn': 'A thing of beauty is a joy forever' and further mocks Wilde with the caption 'What we know *you* know, he is going to let *us* know, you know.' Wilde, the caricature claims, is nothing more than a warmed-over Romantic (echoing the negative reviews levelled against the book of poems he had published in 1881) with nothing original to say.

A series of 1882 lithographs by E.B. Duval entitled 'National Aesthetics' depicts Wilde even more pointedly as an effeminate foreign threat (Figure 5). In this series of five prints, Wilde is drawn as an Irish leprechaun, a German farmer, a Jewish merchant, an African pickaninny and a Chinese man in Mandarin dress. Each print portrays Wilde in crudely stereotypical terms: the German Wilde, for instance, is fat and dim-looking, the Jewish Wilde wears patriotic dress as a desperate attempt to assimilate and sports a long nose, and the African Wilde has ape-like features. Wilde's aesthetics become conflated with fears about increased immigration – the 1880 U.S. Census records over six million immigrants having entered the country in the previous decade –[14] and the racist ideology that rewrites Darwin's theory of degeneration as both a feminizing and a foreign impulse. Bram Dijkstra writes that 'the development

14 U.S. Census Bureau, 'Table 1. Nativity of the Population and Place of Birth of the Native Population: 1850 to 1990,' <http://www.census.gov/population/www/documentation/twps0029/tab01.html>.

Figure 4. 'The British Fungus and the *Wild* American Sunflowers.' *Harper's Weekly* 1882. Oscar Wilde and His Literary Circle. William Andrews Clark Memorial Library, University of California, Los Angeles.

Figure 5. E.B. Duval. 'National Aesthetics.' 1882. Oscar Wilde and His Literary Circle. William Andrews Clark Memorial Library, University of California, Los Angeles.

of woman in general tended to parallel that of the "inferior" races than the evolving white male.'[15] It is not a coincidence then that these caricatures conflate racialist, xenophobic and misogynist views in their depiction of Wilde, and not Oscar Wilde *per se*, but rather the image based on the Sarony photographs that the American press utilized as a generalized sign of a threatening foreign Other.

Perhaps the fear of degeneration was most effectively (if noxiously) depicted in Currier and Ives' lithograph 'The Aesthetic Craze' (Figure 6). The picture portrays Wilde as a thick-lipped black dandy dressed in a shabby version of the knee breeches and velvet coat that Wilde wore while posing for the Sarony photographs. He carries an oversized sunflower and speaks to a black washerwoman while the young maid stops her work to gaze lovingly at him. The lithograph bears the caption 'What's de matter wid de Nigga? Why Oscar you's gone wild!' Currier and Ives use racist pidgin language to draw a connection between the aesthete and the degenerated, atavistic races. Wilde draws these women away from work and lulls them into sensual contemplation (both the oversized sunflower and the enchanted looks on the women's faces attest to this). If work and progress is seen as the sign of white civilization, then Wilde, by focusing attention away from work and into art, represents a form of primitivism that taps into the fears of an increasingly diverse American cultural landscape.

The image of Wilde as a heterosexual, and ultimately powerless, roué disseminated quickly into American popular culture. Wilde as a lascivious satyr became an increasingly popular image since it simultaneously parodied the notion of Wilde as effeminate and exploited the fear that the aesthete might forever prejudice women against more properly masculine men. The mock ballad 'Oscar Dear!,' written by M.H. Rosenfeld and issued in 1882 by Cincinnati

15 Bram Dijkstra, *Idols of Perversity: Fantasies of Feminine Evil in Fin-de-Siècle Culture* (New York: Oxford University Press, 1986), 167.

Figure 6. Currier and Ives. 'The Aesthetic Craze.' 1882. Oscar Wilde and His Literary Circle. William Andrews Clark Memorial Library, University of California, Los Angeles.

exploited the fear that the aesthete might forever prejudice women against more properly masculine men. The mock ballad 'Oscar Dear!,' written by M.H. Rosenfeld and issued in 1882 by Cincinnati publisher F.W. Helmick depicts a walk taken by Wilde and a young girl. As the girl listens to Wilde speaking about art, she also finds that she has to fend off his sexual advances:

> She thought of nothing else but joy,
> Until, just at her side,
> She felt a 'something' softly creep
> And gently there abide.[16]

The refrain 'Oscar, dear, Oscar dear! Take your hand away, sir,' makes light of Wilde as a seducer, but implies the danger he might become should a young women not be so vigilant. This suggestion is reinforced by the cover page of the songsheet, in which a caricature of Wilde in Sarony dress gazes idly at a lily while his hand tickles a young woman's face; the young woman tilts her chin away from his hand and interlaces her fingers over her pubic area in a defensive gesture (Figure 7).

What is particularly interesting about the images of Wilde in the early 1880s is the link the press makes between speaking about art and sexuality, from Maudle's sensual poses to the thrall of the various female audiences to the directly sexual nature of the Currier and Ives' lithograph and the Rosenfeld song. While much of the press made the expected sophomoric connections between art and sexuality, Wilde eventually explored this connection much more thoughtfully in both 'The Portrait of Mr. W.H.' and *The Picture of Dorian Gray*, looking at the erotic dimension, overt or subtle, of a performance. Ironically, Wilde's lectures which began this spate of images in the American press, were not lofty theories about aesthetics,

16 M.H. Rosenfeld, 'Oscar Dear!' Oscar Wilde and His Literary Circle. William Andrews Clark Memorial Library, University of California, Los Angeles.

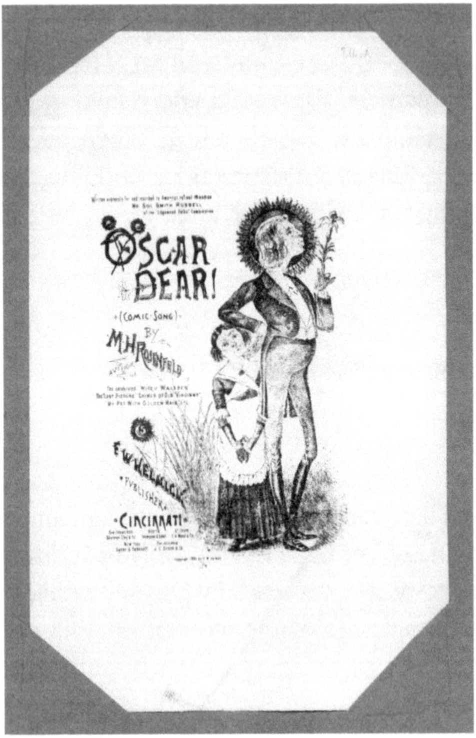

Figure 7. 'Oscar, Dear!' William Andrews Clark Memorial Library, University of California, Los Angeles.

Dorian Gray, looking at the erotic dimension, overt or subtle, of a performance. Ironically, Wilde's lectures which began this spate of images in the American press, were not lofty theories about aesthetics, but consisted of more practical advice and ideas about dress and home decoration; one lecture, which Wilde also delivered in London in a slightly revamped form, was titled 'The House Beautiful.' The reviewer of *The West Middlesex Advertiser* noted that Wilde's London lecture resisted the image circulating in the press. The reviewer comments:

> Those who went to the lecture with any expectation of hearing Mr. Wilde expound any aesthetic theories must have been completely disillusioned before he had spoken ten minutes, for his remarks were eminently practical and descriptive, clearly expressed in pure forcible language, at times poetical, often humorous, and in no single instance obscure, affected, or transcendental. Indeed, no casual visitor entering the hall, and seeing the tall, young gentleman in ordinary evening dress would have imagined that he was the much ridiculed prophet of Aestheticism, nor is this to be wondered at, considering that in no one respect does he resemble the senseless and stupid caricatures of which he has been the victim.[17]

Wilde's career as a writer and his celebrity status bear the marks of a struggle over his persona, since regardless of the changes in Wilde's public image or in the increasing depth and sophistication of his work, the picture of the aesthete in knee breeches making silly and sometimes unhealthy pronouncements about art would loom over his works (to the point of retroactively justifying his guilty verdict for gross indecency). Aware of this but not yet established as a writer, Wilde attempted to exploit the press' negative attention by using existing celebrities and especially famous actresses as vehicles for his work. Ironically, part of his public worship of actresses contributed

17 *The West Middlesex Advertiser*, 14 July 1883. Oscar Wilde and His Literary Circle. William Andrews Clark Memorial Library, University of California, Los Angeles.

in part to the connection the press made between Wilde and women, since his acolyte persona precedes his first American tour.

Gravitating towards these female celebrities seemed to be an almost instinctive move for Wilde, who, as the recurring images of him pointed out, found in women a more sympathetic audience for his aesthetic philosophies. In addition, these famous women, like Wilde, were also engaged in a struggle with the press over their public personae. Yet, unlike Wilde, their unconventional careers and lifestyle choices were cause for admiration rather than ridicule, particularly because their status as performing women emphasized artifice as a way of playing rather than as a way of being. Performance afforded these women a safe space from which they could be distanced from the expectations on their gender and treated sometimes as androgynous models of art. By writing poems and reviews about Sarah Bernhardt and Lillie Langtry, Wilde helped to transform these women from celebrities into icons. But in turn, their status as famous women helped to legitimize his writings and his position as an aesthete.

Although Wilde respectfully extended his compliments to male actors such as Henry Irving and Johnston Forbes-Robertson, he solicited advice from and gave advice to, had dinner with, and showed a greater spirit of camaraderie towards the actresses. He wrote poems in honour of Ellen Terry, collaborated on verse with Helena Modjeska, flattered Mary Anderson into taking the lead in his play *The Duchess of Padua*, and corresponded frequently with actresses such as Genevieve Ward, Mrs. Bernard Beere, and Marie Bancroft. In his biography of Wilde, Hesketh Pearson implies that Wilde consorted with these actresses because he needed women's support to promote his own career.[18] The relationships between Wilde and his actress friends were in fact far more mutually bene-

18 Hesketh Pearson, *Oscar Wilde: His Life and Wit* (New York: Harper and Bros., 1946), 40.

ficial. The actresses may have raised his public profile and helped to solidify his aesthete's persona, but his reviews and poetic tributes also helped to bolster the fame of these women. When Wilde threw an armful of lilies at Sarah Bernhardt's feet or portrayed Terry's performance of Queen Henrietta Maria as a Pre-Raphaelite heroine, he recast these women as works of art, their performances able to inspire works of art in others.[19]

Wilde exploited the link noticed by Rhonda K. Garelick between the dandy's performed masculinity and the actress' performed femininity.[20] The actress' performances emphasized the artifice of her gendered behaviour, an artifice that canny interpreters such as Wilde elevated to an art form. Furthermore, by following the actress' example, Wilde became more sceptical of an impermeable boundary separating private and public selves. Wilde's relationship with Sarah Bernhardt exemplified his attempt to engage in both Bernhardt's cultivation of her public persona and the cultivation of his own. Bernhardt was inspirational in Wilde's development of his theory of performance. She achieved iconic status by subverting traditional ideas of femininity and included androgynous elements in her performances. For Wilde, Bernhardt proved that the most powerful performance crosses gender, class and sexual boundaries. His relationship with Bernhardt is characterized by his attempt to position his own performance in relation to hers.

Of all the actresses enjoying fame in the early 1880s, Sarah Bernhardt arguably occupied a distinct place in the public eye. Bernhardt was thought to have integrated so seamlessly her private life and her public performances that she was seen as the very icon of theatricality. A writer for the *London Times* described her as

19 See Oscar Wilde, 'Queen Henrietta Maria,' in *The Complete Works of Oscar Wilde*, 778 (New York: Barnes and Noble, 1994).

20 Rhonda K. Garelick, *Rising Star: Dandyism, Gender, and Performance in the Fin de Siècle* (Princeton: Princeton University Press, 1998), 6.

> nothing if not original, and her originality, moreover, fantastic thought it may be, is never without a certain magnetic power or fascination that rivets the attention and sometimes even warps the judgment of the spectator.[21]

Paradoxically, Bernhardt embodied theatricality by subverting the conventions of femininity actresses were supposed to uphold in their performances. She was unfashionably thin, almost wraith-like, she was not attractive in the traditional sense, and she flaunted her unconventional lifestyle, which included posing for a series of nude photographs early in her career.[22]

When she toured London for the second time in 1879, Bernhardt's persona was being dissected and analyzed by the British literati and press. The newspapers faithfully recounted her gross income, expenditures and financial ephemera such as how much money she would have to pay customs to allow her to bring her costumes on a tour of the United States.[23] Her success was such that various writers attempted to define the qualities that made her so compelling an actress. Henry James, for instance, dismissed her performances as media courtship, calling her the 'muse of the newspaper' and claiming, 'She is a celebrity because, apparently, she desires with an intensity that has rarely been equalled to be one, and because for this end all means are alike to her.'[24] A writer for the *London Times*, on the other hand, implied that Bernhardt's fame was the result of living (as a Jewish woman and the daughter of a courtesan) on the fringes of social acceptability.[25] Bernhardt's fame

---

21 *London Times*, 5 July 1884.

22 Arthur Gold and Sir Robert Fizdale, *The Divine Sarah: A Life of Sarah Bernhardt* (New York: Knopf, 1991), 64.

23 *London Times*, 13 December 1880.

24 Henry James, *The Scenic Art: Notes on Acting and the Drama 1872–1901*, ed. Allan Wade (New York: Hill and Wang, 1957), 129.

25 *London Times*, 3 July 1879.

obfuscated her social marginality; at the same time, however, her fame also transformed her marginality into a virtue.

Like Wilde, the actress in the late nineteenth century was subject to a double perception. The stage was one of the only areas where women could equal and in some cases exceed the salary and status of her male counterparts.[26] Moreover, the stage gave the successful actress the possibility of managing her own company, thereby retaining even more control over her income. Bernhardt, for example, managed her own acting company for a short period of time. But the life of an actress could still be morally suspect. The notion of a woman putting herself on display in front of a paying public often too easily slipped into a comparison with, if not outright to the prostitute, then to the adventuress. Some of the most popular actresses of the time therefore found a way to construct personae that were sufficiently removed from their personal lives and powerful enough to substitute for a private revelation of themselves. Ellen Terry, for instance, was identified throughout her career as the ideal English woman and enjoyed tremendous success based upon that persona despite the fact that she had divorced her husband and lived out of wedlock with architect E.W. Godwin for many years, bearing him two children.[27]

Bernhardt, on the other hand, achieved notoriety by having her public persona influence her 'private' one. She took care to have her offstage behaviour recorded in the press, providing the public with outrageous acts that could be reconciled easily with the melodramatic characters she often played. In one much-publicized occurrence, the press told of Bernhardt having read a scandalous book written by a rival actress which portrayed Bernhardt in less than

26 Michael R. Booth, *Theatre in the Victorian Age* (Cambridge: Cambridge University Press, 1991), 112.

27 See Nina Auerbach, *Ellen Terry: Player in Her Time* (Philadelphia: University of Pennsylvania Press, 1987).

flattering terms. According to the *London Times*, Bernhardt barged into her rival's home and beat her with a cane, after which she presented the cane to the apartment house's porter, stating that it was a gift for her rival. Rather than chastising Bernhardt for unladylike behaviour, the *Times* applauded her actions.[28]

Moreover, by the early 1880s, an actress such as Bernhardt, who relied heavily on her physical presence, benefitted enormously from the change in theatrical lighting. In 1881, D'Oyly Carte converted his Savoy Theatre from gas to electric lighting. Gas lighting had cast the entire theatre in a diffused light; the new electric light allowed for a darkened house, with all the light focused on the stage.[29] The resulting demarcation of performers from spectators allowed the actor to display seemingly transcendental qualities. The actor, thrown into sharp relief by the intense concentration of light, was scrutinized for his or her physical appearance and vocal ability as part of his or her craft. The image he or she projected became an integral part of judging acting ability.

Such attention to the physicality of actors gave them a common bond with those offstage performers, the dandies and aesthetes of the late Victorian period. Since the Regency, the dandy used costume and mannerisms to present a theatricalised persona, commenting on social norms by purporting to disdain them. Charles Baudelaire remarks that 'the word "dandy" implies a quintessence of character and a subtle understanding of the entire moral mechanism of the world.'[30] The dandy, by virtue of his cultivation of himself, rejected the notion of being part of a social mass and proclaimed that the expression of his individuality was an art form.[31] The aes-

28 *London Times*, 3 July 1879.

29 Wolf von Eckhardt, Sander L. Gilman and J. Edward Chamberlin, *Oscar Wilde's London: A Scrapbook of Vices and Virtues 1890–1900* (Garden City, NY: Anchor Press, 1987), 54.

30 Baudelaire, 'The Painter of Modern Life,' 9.

31 Ellen Moers, *The Dandy: Brummell to Beerbohm* (New York: Viking, 1960), 265.

thetes of the early 1880s synthesized dandyish self-presentation with Pater's more ethereal notion that self-cultivation could function as an interpretive force. Returning to Wilde's early inquiries at Oxford, self-cultivation was important in so far as it can inspire a similar effort towards self-cultivation in others.

Even more than her male counterpart, the actress provided a link to the dandy-aesthete in that her performed femininity was figured as artificial as the dandy's performed masculinity. To be feminine in the late Victorian period meant performing one's gender as an act of concealment, by disavowing the social construction embedded within the performance. Wilde would later exploit this paradoxical action in *The Importance of Being Earnest* when Gwendolen and Cecily constantly make ironic the feminine coding underlying their actions.

Wilde may have appropriated many aspects of feminine performance, but his attitudes toward actresses were also tinged with the aesthete's tendency to view these actresses as static works of art. Ultimately, the actress' performance was most valuable as a catalyst for Wilde to write criticism and poetry, merging his own persona with that of a particular actress in his writings. Bernhardt's greatest gift to Wilde, for example, was allowing him to demonstrate publicly the acolyte's artistic manipulations of his idol. Self-cultivation remained at the heart of Wilde's explorations into these women's personae. At Oxford, he outlined the possibility of a persona conveying meaning through performance; in London in the early 1880s, he explored the practical applications of this theory.

Celebrity in the late nineteenth century, whether it was on the scale of Bernhardt's renown or on the smaller scale of Wilde's increased public exposure, thrived on a somewhat vexed relationship between the display and concealment of socially questionable traits. Hannah Arendt in *The Origins of Totalitarianism* describes late nineteenth-century society as an environment where the socially marginalized could gain widespread recognition and acceptance if they presented themselves as a notable exception to their gender, class or ethnicity. The socially marginalized could therefore gain entrance into the *salons* of the upper classes by performing their social differences. She writes,

> The role of the inverts was to show their abnormality, of the Jews to represent black magic ('necromancy'), of the artists to manifest another form of supernatural and superhuman contact, of the aristocrats to show that they were not like ordinary ('bourgeois') people.[32]

Through their performances, a Jewish actress such as Bernhardt and an Irish aesthete such as Wilde could become famous by performing an easily-identifiable persona to society. The persona comes to represent the individual in his or her entirety, and the individual is accepted because by performing the assumptions regarding his or her cultural background, he or she manages to transcend them. Both Wilde and Bernhardt were able to accomplish this seemingly contradictory feat. Bernhardt achieved fame by combining the foreignness of the Jew made mysterious by French and British stereotypes with the cult of the dying woman she exploited in plays like Racine's *Phèdre* and Dumas *fils' La dame aux camélias.* Wilde combined Pater's ethereal aesthetic theory with the rapier wit of the dandy. Bernhardt's physical presence and her fierce independence were seen as representative of her modernity. And Wilde's dandified costumes and wit cast him as the epitome of the aesthete.

According to her memoir *My Double Life*, when Bernhardt disembarked from the ship in 1879, ready to begin her London engagement, Wilde cast a bouquet of lilies at her feet and shouted, '*Vive* Sarah Bernhardt!'[33] Shortly afterwards, Wilde invited Bernhardt was to the apartments he shared with artist Frank Miles. William Ward

32 Hannah Arendt, *The Origins of Totalitarianism* (New York: Harcourt Brace, 1975), 85.

33 Sarah Bernhardt, *My Double Life*, trans. Victoria Tietze Larson (Albany: State University of New York Press, 1999), 204.

heard the details of the evening from Wilde: Bernhardt scribbled her name on a wall and practiced high-kicking in front of Wilde and Miles.[34] Their relationship was never a camaraderie of peers; Bernhardt later remembered Wilde as 'a devoted attendant, [who] did much to make things pleasant and easy for me in London, but he never appeared to pay court.'[35]

To Wilde, Bernhardt was a modern manifestation of Pater's Mona Lisa, a work of art whose presence could spur her critics to new heights of creativity. Indeed, Bernhardt embodied many of the qualities of performance Wilde had been exploring since his Oxford days. Also, her persona was so powerful that it influenced the critical reception of her performances. Theatre reviewers at the time often criticized Bernhardt for a lack of variation in her performances. Her voice droned, her gestures were static, and her interpretations of the different characters she played were strikingly similar.[36] Rather than being an impediment to her acting reputation, however, the sameness of her performances worked because they ended up reinforcing her bizarre but captivating persona.

In her honour, Wilde wrote a sonnet, 'Phèdre,' which, though ostensibly about Bernhardt's performance in the Racine tragedy, focuses almost exclusively on her persona.[37] The sonnet captures the morbidity Bernhardt projected as an important part of her persona and the death imagery in the poem specifically references Bernhardt rather than the tragic character she plays.[38] For instance,

34 W.W. Ward, 'Oscar Wilde: An Oxford Reminiscence,' in *Oscar Wilde: Interviews and Recollections*, ed. E.H. Mikhail, 12–15 (London: Macmillan, 1979), 14.

35 Ellmann, *Oscar Wilde*, 118.

36 See John Stokes, Michael Booth and Susan Bassnett, *Bernhardt, Terry, Duse: The Actress in Her Time* (Cambridge: Cambridge University Press, 1988), 12.

37 'Phèdre' was published in *The World* on 11 June 1879. See Ellmann, *Oscar Wilde*, 118.

38 Ruth Brandon, *Being Divine: A Biography of Sarah Bernhardt* (London: Mandarin, 1992), 188.

the description of Bernhardt as having 'loveless lips with which men kiss in Hell' evokes the photographs of her lying corpse-like in a coffin.[39] In 'Phèdre,' Bernhardt is presented as the perfect synthesis of the classical and modern spirits, the figure of one who 'gathered reeds from a green stream / For Goat-foot Pan's shrill piping,' who also embodies a sense of modern despair.[40] Like Pater's Mona Lisa, Bernhardt in 'Phèdre' is at once surface representation and abstract suggestion. Moreover, the poem describes a classical environment befitting an ephebe. Wilde imagines Bernhardt walking through the groves of the Greek Academy. Bernhardt as portrayed by Wilde is also both Phaedra and Hippolytus, incorporating the ephebic youth into the performance of the passionate widow.

Bernhardt doesn't figure that explicitly in Wilde's writing at the time of their friendship (although later she would be the inspiration for Salome), yet her persona helped him to refine his aesthetic theories. His lecture 'The English Renaissance of Art,' delivered on 9 January 1882 in New York, invokes persona as a correlative to aestheticism. 'The English Renaissance of Art' echoes Wilde's treatment of Bernhardt as muse and model. In the lecture, Wilde stresses the importance of looking at the work of art as if one were watching a dramatic performance. The critic seeks to define beauty in terms as concrete as he is able to imagine, while still acknowledging that much of what comprises beauty is incommunicable and grounded in the work of art itself:

> For it is not enough that a work of art should conform to the aesthetic demands of its age: there must be also about it, if it is to affect us with any permanent delight, the impress of a distinct individuality, an individuality remote from that of ordinary men, and coming near to us only by virtue of a

39 Oscar Wilde, 'Phèdre,' in *Complete Works*, 777.

40 Ibid.

> certain newness and wonder in the work, and through channels whose very strangeness makes us more ready to give them welcome.[41]

Each work of art, according to Wilde, radiates a persona which can affect an audience in the same visceral way as the persona of a stage performer. In a process reminiscent of twentieth-century phenomenology, the critic's task is to understand the artwork's persona by utilizing his own persona to interpret it. He writes, 'It is for the critic to teach the people how to find in the calm of such art the highest expression of their own stormy passions.'[42] In addition, the work of art is feminized. Wilde calls all great art 'delicate art, roughness having little to do with strength, and harshness very little to do with power.'[43] The masculine work of art criticism allows the art's feminized persona to almost erotically permeate it, the result of which is a birth of a new form of creativity. Just as Bernhardt's performance inspired critics to write about her in terms of their impressions of the effects she produced, Wilde exhorts his audience to treat the work of art in the same fashion. Wilde writes in 'The English Renaissance of Art': '*La personalité*, said one of the greatest modern French critics, *voilà ce qui nous sauvera.*'[44]

Bernhardt's outsized personality did not save Wilde, but she was one of two women who helped him see the correlations between theatricality, aesthetics and performativity. The other, arguably more important, influence was Lillie Langtry, whom Wilde was introduced to by Frank Miles in 1879. Langtry had been a celebrity in London since her appearance at a party during the 1877 social season where she wore a shockingly simple black dress and

41 Oscar Wilde, 'The English Renaissance of Art,' in *The Uncollected Oscar Wilde*, ed. John Wyse Jackson, 3–28 (London: Fourth Estate Limited, 1995), 9.

42 Ibid., 18.

43 Ibid., 21.

44 Ibid., 9. The English translation of the phrase reads: 'The personality – this is who will save us.'

caused an immediate stir among the artists in attendance, Miles and John Everett Millais among them. Both Miles and Millais engaged her services as a model and soon afterwards she became known throughout London as a Professional Beauty, her picture appearing for sale on postcards in London shops and newsstands. Professional Beauties were usually upper-class women whose photographs (without remuneration, of course) were purchased by usually middle-class collectors. Langtry, however, was not a traditional Professional Beauty in this sense; she was the daughter of a Jersey clergyman whose husband was heavily in debt. She used her Professional Beauty status and her love affair with the Prince of Wales to enter upper-class social circles, to obtain credit from the fashionable London shops, and to maintain a lifestyle which her husband's income could not afford her.

Wilde and Langtry struck up a fast friendship based on both mutual admiration and mutual benefit, and soon he was seen accompanying her in the London streets, carrying lilies to her doorstep and praising her attributes to everyone whom he encountered. He took pride in his friendship with the most celebrated woman in London society and frequently mentioned Langtry's name to acquaintances. In a letter to Harold Boulton in 1879, he writes, 'I was very sorry you did not come to tea as I could have introduced you to some very beautiful people. Mrs. Langtry and Lady Lonsdale and a lot of clever beings who were at tea with me.'[45] He saw Langtry, another middle-class person striving to fit in to the upper classes, as a Galatea figure and, as much as he played the adoring acolyte, he also tried to reshape her into his living work of art, the embodiment of his still-developing theories about persona and art.

Scholars have been divided over the nature of Langtry and Wilde's relationship. Richard Ellmann, for instance, argues that

---

45 Oscar Wilde, *Complete Letters*, 86–87.

Langtry was very much a creation of Wilde's.[46] Hesketh Pearson, on the other hand, claims that, although Wilde attempted to remake Langtry, these efforts were met by considerable resistance and often failure.[47] Like Bernhardt, Langtry was never solely Wilde's creation, her persona never restricted to Wilde's utterances about her. Unlike Bernhardt, however, Wilde was a direct contributor to the Langtry persona, helping to shape her image and, by doing so, giving his ideas a greater public forum and legitimizing himself as a critic. Langtry most notably embodied Wilde's later dictum in 'The Critic as Artist': 'To arrive at what one really believes, one must speak through lips different from one's own.'[48] As a woman, Langtry physically occupied a position which Wilde could only play with imaginatively and, as a woman noted only for her beauty, she could become the art object to Wilde's artist and show off *his* creative prowess in the dresses he selected for her and the mannerisms he taught her.

Frank Miles reportedly crowed upon seeing Langtry, 'I with my pencil, Oscar with his pen, will make her the Joconde and Laura of this century.'[49] It was an understanding between the two men that Miles would immortalize Langtry in picture and Wilde would do the same for her in print. H. Montgomery Hyde goes so far as to suggest that the Langtry phenomenon was the result of an active collaboration between Miles and Wilde.[50] Miles did sell several sketches of Langtry to magazines. And several of Wilde's poems during this period are dedicated explicitly to Langtry, among them 'Madonna Mia,' in which the 'fair slim boy' of an earlier draft metamorphoses

46 Ellmann, *Oscar Wilde*, 114.

47 Pearson, *Oscar Wilde*. 48.

48 Oscar Wilde, 'The Critic as Artist,' in *The Soul of Man*, 263.

49 Pearson, *Oscar Wilde*, 48.

50 H. Montgomery Hyde, *Oscar Wilde* (New York: Farrar, Straus and Giroux, 1975), 41.

into 'A lily-girl, not made for this world's pain' in the published version.[51]

During their friendship, Wilde not only advised Langtry on how to dress for the parties which demanded her to be as much a fashion plate as a beauty, he also tutored her in Latin and Greek and led her on museum outings. In one notable outing, Wilde brought her to Newton's lectures on Greek art at the British Museum; another museum outing sees them looking for Greek coins which capture the likeness of Sarah Bernhardt.[52] Although he preferred to play in public the role of the doting admirer, his imagining of himself as Pygmalion was always and not-so-subtly lurking beneath his surface adoration. Langtry's resentment about being Wilde's model often led to tension in their friendship. Although Wilde's complaints about Langtry's resistance had his tongue firmly in his cheek, he could not resist his desire to treat the women in his life as art objects; he would later choose his wife Constance's outfits for formal occasions and help her in styling her new outfits when she became an advocate for the Rational Dress Movement.[53] Wilde and Langtry were often seen walking the streets of London in matching or complementary outfits. These promenades linked Langtry and Wilde together in the public eye as a matched set. In letters, Langtry was constantly the guest of honour at his teas, the muse to his artist, the beauty to his wit, the creation to his creativity. His poems to her further solidify this particular interpretation of their friendship. The

---

51 Wilde, 'Madonna Mia,' in *Complete Works*, 777.

52 Lillie Langtry, *The Days I Knew* (New York: George H. Doran, 1925), 92.

53 Wilde's sense of humour during this period when he is being caricatured as the aesthete is shown here when he writes to a friend: 'The lily is so tiresome …She *won't* do what I tell her… I assure her that she owes it to herself and to us to drive daily through the Park dressed entirely in black, in a black victoria drawn by black horses, and with 'Venus Annodomini' emblazoned on her black bonnet in dull sapphires, but she won't do it.' Rpt. in James Brough, *The Prince and the Lily* (London: Hodder and Stoughton, 1975), 187.

Langtry character in these poems is always removed in a sense from the world, whether as a dying girl, a goddess, or a parting lover, and requires exegesis by the one person capable of a thorough and sincere devotion to her.

Although Langtry referred to Wilde as her 'kind tutor' in her memoir *The Days I Knew*, she downplayed his role in her social success, noting his many adoring gestures but little of the actual tutelage which had taken place.[54] She takes nearly complete credit for creating her public image, but concedes that Wilde 'possessed a remarkably fascinating and compelling personality, and what in an actor would be termed wonderful "stage presence."'[55] Furthermore, Wilde was a model for everyday performance. Langtry writes, 'His affectations, I may say, were mainly for the benefit of the general public. To his friends he always remained the same.'[56] Laura Beatty, however, argues that Langtry consciously absorbs Wilde's ideas about personality into her public persona.[57] Langtry's letters during this period bear an unmistakable similarity to Wilde's prose style. In a letter to Wilde, she writes that she wore 'a soft black Greek dress with a fringe of silver crescents and stars, and diamond ones in my hair and on my neck, and called it Queen of Night.'[58] As Langtry became more famous, Wilde's association with her increased his own celebrity. Langtry's visits meant that on more than one occasion the Prince of Wales would be present as well, which guaranteed him a measure of publicity. Langtry's acceptance into upper-class society because of her liaison with the Prince was of immense help to Wilde, since artists without aristocratic connections were not normally welcomed into these circles.

---

54 Hyde, *Oscar Wilde*, 40.

55 Langtry, *The Days I Knew*, 83.

56 Ibid., 85.

57 Laura Beatty, *Lillie Langtry: Manners, Masks and Morals* (London: Chatto and Windus, 1999), 234.

58 Wilde, *Complete Letters*, 92*n*.

For Wilde, Langtry's public persona was a measure not just of celebrity but of exploring possibilities for the performance of one's identity, specifically a gender identity that Wilde was being criticized by the press with having betrayed. Marvin Carlson succinctly sums up the importance of gender performance to Wilde. Carlson writes that for Wilde, 'performance clearly provided a strategy for the social construction of an identity that permitted the integration of a normally troubling amount of "female" characteristics into a "male" persona.'[59] This statement can be better understood in light of Judith Butler's contention that gender is 'a set of repeated acts within a highly rigid regulatory frame that congeal over time to produce the appearance of substance, of a natural sort of being.'[60] Wilde learned early in his career that gender itself is a performative practice and he later makes this plain in his writings and in his interest in androgynous figures, such as Salome, Dorian Gray, and the Shakespearean boy actor Willie Hughes. Langtry's appeal derived from projecting a feminine persona with tantalizing masculine qualities, as Laura Beatty notes:

> Her appetites were pronounced and dark. Her looks were heavy and sometimes masculine. She had the physical dash and daring of her brothers. She could swim and row and ride. She had a frankness about her and a boyish grace. And yet she was a woman.[61]

She is in this sense a perfect complement to Wilde's effeminate persona.

Not long after his friendship with Langtry began, Wilde made a point of coming to call on her while carrying an amaryllis. He caused

59 Marvin Carlson, *Performance: A Critical Introduction* (London: Routledge, 1996), 155.

60 Judith Butler, *Gender Trouble: Feminism and the Subversion of Identity* (New York: Routledge, 1990), 33.

61 Beatty, *Lillie Langtry*, 141.

a stir in the United States by casting a bouquet of lilies onto the ground when Langtry arrived in New York. On one notorious evening, Langtry's husband, coming home late at night, nearly tripped over a sleeping Wilde. The press responded to Wilde's public performance as Langtry's devoted disciple by mockingly casting Wilde as a male version of the Professional Beauty. An article in the *Boston Post* in May 1881 jeers:

> Mrs. Langtry and the other professional beauties of London have a rival in the shape of a beautiful youth named Oscar Wilde, a poet and an aesthetic. His picture adorns all the shop windows and is even taken in the aesthetic style with a bunch of lilies in his hand. He must look as lovely as a yellow cat having a fit in a dish of stewed tomatoes.[62]

Despite the mockery of Wilde from journalists such as the one above, which Wilde had probably expected, his association with Langtry was helping to cement his reputation as an aesthete. In turn, his writings about her were reinforcing her status as an icon of beauty despite some of her shortcomings. For instance, Wilde, having encouraged Langtry to capitalize on her fame and begin an acting career, was hired by the *New York World* in 1882 to review Langtry's production of Tom Taylor's *An Unequal Match*. In this review, he comments favourably on Langtry's appearance and dress, commends the production values – in short, he speaks of everything but the play and Langtry's performance.[63] The review also emphasizes Wilde's particular vision of Langtry's beauty, linking it again to the Greek ideals he was so committed to disseminating to the Victorian public: 'Pure Greek [Langtry's beauty] is, with the grave low forehead, the exquisitely arched brow; the noble chiselling of the mouth,

---

62 Ernest Dudley, *The Gilded Lily: The Life and Loves of the Fabulous Lillie Langtry* (London: Oldhams Press, 1958), 18.

63 See Wilde, 'Mrs. Langtry as Hester Grazebrook,' in *The Uncollected Oscar Wilde*, 67–70.

shaped as if it were the mouthpiece of an instrument of music…'[64] The review is mostly a reiteration of Wilde's public pronouncements of Langtry's beauty, but it is also a piece of his speaking performances put into print, at once hyperbolic and insightful.

Langtry occupied a crucial position at this point in Wilde's career, serving as what Erving Goffman calls a 'front.' According to Goffman, every performance, theatrical or not, is a citation of an already-constructed dialogue between performer and audience. In order for a performance to be legible to its audience, certain prior expectations must be met.[65] Wilde was in a sense creating his own front in the early 1880s by shaping the popular image of the aesthete as he was performing it. But Langtry gave a certain tangibility to this construction. Whereas Wilde's oral and written performances in the press relied on the front of the idealistic aesthete, the image of him carrying a lily in the street in honour of Langtry created the public's expectations of Wilde far more strongly than his own sayings and quips did.

What became important in Wilde's writings about Langtry was not her beauty, but the way in which he describes her, compares her, deduces and induces her – in short, how she as a subject allows him to develop his critical and artistic spirit. His poem 'The New Helen' was published in the *World* in 1879.[66] Wilde presented Langtry his tribute to her beauty with a vellum-bound copy which both flattered and irritated her. Langtry recalled,

> When he was writing *The New Helen* he became so obsessed with the subject that he would walk round and round the streets in which our little house was situated for hours at a time, probably investing me with every quality I never

64 Ibid., 67.

65 Erving Goffman, *The Presentation of Self in Everyday Life* (Woodstock, NY: Overlook Press, 1973), 22.

66 Dudley, *The Gilded Lily*, 17.

possessed, and although Wilde had a keen sense of the ridiculous, he sometimes unconsciously bordered thereon himself.[67]

Yet she included the poem in its entirety in *The Days I Knew*. It is not altogether surprising that Langtry was of two minds about 'The New Helen.' On the surface, the poem is an elaborate, over-the-top publicization of Langtry's beauty. Indeed, two years prior to the publication of 'The New Helen,' *Vanity Fair* proclaimed that Langtry 'still awaits a poet to make her known' and the poem is on the surface a fitting tribute by the artist to his muse.[68] However, the relationship between the artist and his muse is revealed in the poem's ambivalences, some of which Langtry seems to have picked up on.

The poem begins with an image of a femme fatale returning to the chaos she had initially caused:

Where hast thou been since round the walls of Troy
The sons of God fought in that great emprise?
Why dost thou walk our common earth again?[69]

The words are a reproof. The poem's initial image depicts the power of art to overwhelm men and evoke extraordinary actions. Helen, as the embodiment of beauty, shirks her duty by her absence but her return is also a reminder in the poem that her beauty and the destruction she causes are one and the same. Indeed, the Helen of this poem is a precursor to Wilde's later *fatale* characters, Dorian Gray and Salome, and the linking of beauty and destruction as two sides of the same powerful force is a theme he returns to in his fairy tales as well.

Indeed, Wilde veers away in the poem from Helen's beauty to the suffering which her beauty causes. In the fourth stanza, however, he turns from Helen to Odysseus' wanderings. He recasts

---

67 Langtry, *The Days I Knew*, 92–93.

68 *Vanity Fair*, 19 May 1877.

69 Wilde, 'The New Helen,' in *Complete Works*, 733.

Odysseus' journey as the search for Helen, who Wilde transforms from the initial narrative cause of his journey to the aesthetic catalyst of a muse. Thus the remainder of the poem, while still ostensibly about the power of beauty, focuses mainly on the struggle of the artist to contain his inspiration. Helen becomes a fleeting, temporary image in the latter half of the poem. The remainder of the stanza highlights Wilde's ambivalence concerning his relationship to the art object and his status as an artist:

> But, like that bird, the servant of the sun,
> Who flies before the north wind and the night,
> So wilt thou fly our evil land and drear,
> Back to the tower of thine old delight,
> And the red lips of young Euphorion;
> Nor shall I ever see thy face again,
> But in this poisonous garden close must stay,
> Crowning my brows with the thorn-crown of pain,
> Till all my loveless life shall pass away.[70]

On the one hand, Helen is seen in the clichéd imagery of beauty too pure to exist in the corrupt world. Yet the artist, responsible for bringing beauty into the world, in effect banishes her to the tower. She still exists to torture the artist, now portrayed as a Christ-like figure sacrificing himself for art, but she does so in a confined space. (Wilde here is reversing the central image in Tennyson's 'Lady of Shallott.' The poem, while using the classical subject matter so dear to young poets recently graduated from university, owes much thematically and imagistically to Tennyson's poems.) The stanza reveals the ambivalence which exists at the heart of Wilde's relationship with Langtry. Although he publicly is willing to play the martyr to art, Wilde is actually advocating control over one's art. While art may exist outside of the artist, it is only the artist's per-

70 Ibid., 734.

formance which can make art legible to the public. The artist's muse, no matter how famous, is of secondary importance in this process.

The final stanza directly connects Langtry with Helen. It opens with a contrasting image: 'Lily of love, pure and inviolate! / Tower of ivory! red rose of fire!' and proceeds to glorify her as the modern icon of beauty.[71] The poem turns one last time to the suffering of the devoted, stating that, although Helen's beauty makes the lives of her followers seem bleak in comparison, it is the bleakness reminiscent of Tennyson's 'The Lotos-Eaters,' a 'slumberous anodyne / For wasted lives, for lingering wretchedness.'[72] It would appear that the artist is conceding some sort of aesthetic victory to his art; this victory is made more effective because of its placement at the end of the poem. Wilde acknowledges that between artist and art there is always a struggle for control and he, in the poem as well as in his life, tries to overcome this struggle by fashioning himself as both artist and work of art. In this sense, Langtry's importance diminishes. Regardless of Wilde's glorification of her, she remains of secondary importance to Wilde's cultivation of his own public performance. Likewise Helen, despite her status as beauty personified, is a creation of her devotees, as the final stanza's emphasis suggests.

Langtry served as one of the more important points of reference for Wilde's developing performance as poet and aesthete. Philip Auslander suggests that the performer is in fact an 'intertext,' a point of convergence which can be read through the performance.[73] As a performer, Wilde expresses himself as an aggregate of signs – Hellenic and modern, dandy and earnest teacher of art. Langtry is the focal point through which these signs can be identified and referred back to Wilde. Although he did have a genuine

71 Ibid., 735.

72 Ibid.

73 Auslander, *From Acting to Performance*, 29. Auslander is following Julia Kristeva's theory of intertextuality.

friendship with Langtry and left the touching poem 'To L.L.' as evidence of this relationship, Wilde nonetheless attempted to contain Langtry within the limits of his artistic vision.

After the publication of 'The New Helen,' a parodic songsheet mocking Wilde's association with famous women soon began to circulate in London. 'The Bard of Beauty' was credited to 'Oscuro Mild' and its cover featured an illustration of Wilde flanked by the likenesses of Langtry as the Jersey Lily and Ellen Terry as Portia, a bouquet of lilies piercing his waist and Wilde-faced cherubs descending around him. The song accuses Wilde of being derivative and charges him with emptying poetry of its meaning:

> Fresh metaphors like magi from afar,
> Lit by no star of meaning, to thy feet,
> For these and similar poetic tricks
> Are highly prized our master's school among
> O Swinburne! And O water! how ye mix
> To constitute the modern poet's song.[74]

The claim that Wilde's work was a pose without substance haunted him more than any other artistic charge levelled against him, including plagiarism. Wilde's association with actresses was seen to be nothing more than a superficial grab for celebrity, but it marks the beginning of overturning the surface-depth binary which is at the core of his theory of performance. It took several years, after a stint as a journalist and editor, but Wilde eventually sets forth his anatomy of performance – its makeup, its function, and its importance to both cultural understanding and social betterment.

74 'The Bard of Beauty'. *Time*, April 1880. Oscar Wilde and His Literary Circle. William Andrews Clark Memorial Library, University of California, Los Angeles. 'Swinburne and water' was a phrase coined by the press to mock Wilde's borrowing of the older poet's rhythms.

Chapter Three
Wilde's Performance Theory and the Critical Essays

Although many scholars portray Wilde as having exploited his press coverage to further his own celebrity, the Wilde the media imagined proved to be more of a hindrance than a help to his career. To a certain extent, the press did aid Wilde by establishing him within popular culture; it created a space for Wilde from where his words would be listened to. However, the press' caricatures of Wilde created an expectation that Wilde was not to be taken altogether seriously; that, at worst, he was merely reiterating the ideas of Pater, Whistler or the Romantic poets and, at best, his few good ideas were obfuscated by the dandyish pose he assumed. Unsurprisingly, then, Wilde was ambivalent about his media celebrity. His celebrity increased the public's exposure to his ideas but at the same time he was at the mercy of the press' manipulations of his persona.

As the 1880s progressed, Wilde moved away from his aesthetic persona. Although he returned to the United States for a second lecturing tour and continued to speak about aesthetics in England, he abandoned the knee breeches and velvet capes made famous by the Sarony photographs. By the latter half of the decade, Wilde no longer performed as the 'aesthete.' Instead, he disappeared behind his written work. He wrote over one hundred reviews and articles in the 1880s, mostly on literary, theatrical and artistic subjects, and almost all of them unsigned. In contrast to his much-publicized persona in the early 1880s, the Wilde of the mid-1880s was relatively subdued, to the point where an article in the *Pall Mall Gazette* in 1887 jeered, 'Oscar's star has been low on the horizon since he cut his hair and became "Benedick the married man."'[1] Married to Constance Lloyd in 1884 and a father a year later, he nonetheless retained some aspects of his earlier aesthetic self. Early in his marriage, for instance, he advised Constance on dress and public presentation in a similar fashion as he had done with Lillie Langtry. However, financial concerns brought upon by a growing family caused Wilde in the mid-1880s to spend as much time as possible writing for the newspapers and, as a result, the ostentatious dandy all but disappeared.

In the late 1880s, however, Wilde wrote a series of essays ('The Decay of Lying,' 'The Critic as Artist,' 'The Truth of Masks,' 'Pen, Pencil and Poison,' 'The Soul of Man under Socialism,' and 'The Portrait of Mr. W.H.') which collectively elucidate the performance theory he had been developing since his university days. Evoking again the Hegelian dialectic he had worked with in his early notes on performance, Wilde's essays all share the idea that one's persona develops out of an agonistic relationship between self and other. The dialogues of 'The Decay of Lying' and 'The Critic as Artist' reflect this dialectic, as does his insistence that Wainewright in 'Pen, Pencil and Poison' creates his persona in response to the Romantic image of the criminal as misunderstood artist. In 'The Soul of Man under Socialism,' Wilde extends the relationship between self and other to include the struggle between art and commodification. For Wilde, the dialectic relationship creates a mode of exchange between individuals' personae based upon the erotic desire encoded within the charismatic phenomena of 'fascination' and 'influence.' Anticipating the popularity of psychological theories, Freudian psychoanalysis in particular, Wilde puts forth a concept of individuals whose identities are comprised of different personae, the performances and receptions of which determine cultural development.

Wilde's theory of performance is located at the convergence of his philosophical convictions, his career, and his erotic desire. His

1 Ellmann, *Oscar Wilde*, 281.

theory is an attempt to liberate the concept of the self from ideological expectations. A persona is to him an example of the self at play, donning masks and poses in order to replace the concept of an integrated authentic self with one that privileges multiplicity, performance and the self as work of art. The normative self is an ideological construct that the world of art deliberately resists. As he writes in 'The Critic as Artist,' 'Man is least himself when he talks in his own person. Give him a mask, and he will tell you the truth.'[2] In the struggle between art and a utilitarian society, an individual's persona is art's primary weapon against the tyranny of the normal. To look at the individual in terms of his or her persona necessitates abandoning any preconceived construct of the self, since Wilde's concept of the persona works against the Victorian assumption that the self's primary purpose is to serve the social order.

Drawing on his associations with the acting world and his own experiences writing plays, Wilde's essays 'The Decay of Lying' and 'The Critic as Artist' are not only imitations of Socratic dialogues but are mini-dramas, performances within themselves. Both dialogues feature a lead role (Vivian in 'The Decay of Lying' and Gilbert in 'The Critic as Artist') who use the art of conversation in order to seduce the secondary character into accepting his ideas. After one of Gilbert's assertions in 'The Critic as Artist,' for instance, Ernest responds, 'While you talk it seems to me to be so.'[3] Gilbert's arguments in this case gain their authority by being filtered through his seductive speaking performance, his verbal dexterity enticing Ernest into accepting his ideas.

In the dialogues, the performance is not only as important as the content, it in effect constructs the content. The actors in the essays perform that which they speak and therefore the essays are understood through the performances. For instance, in 'The Critic

2 Wilde, 'The Critic as Artist,' 261.

3 Ibid., 234.

as Artist,' Gilbert muses, 'How exquisite these single daffodils are! They seem to be made of amber and irony. They are like Greek things of the best period.'[4] This interlude of purple prose demonstrates both the power of an aestheticized sensibility to make art out of everyday objects and the way in which Gilbert compels his audience to enter into an aesthetic exchange. 'What was the story in the confessions of the remorseful Academician that made you laugh?' he asks Ernest. 'Tell it to me.'[5] The body of Gilbert's argument is structured by storytelling conventions; through the argument, Gilbert encourages Ernest to structure his response along the same lines.

As Herbert Sussman notes, the dialogues are 'a solo performance in which, to the admiration of the minor character, the principal figure moves from assertion to assertion just as an actor shifts from role to role.'[6] The concept of the dialogues as performance, with their emphasis on summative knowledge rather than deductive or inductive argumentation, subverts both the idea and the purpose of the conventional critical essay. As a result, critics have sometimes charged Wilde's essays with inconsistency and lack of logical rigor. Epifanio San Juan, Jr., for example, claims that the Wilde in these essays 'is not wholly a consistent and systematic thinker.'[7] What critics such as San Juan miss, however, is that the dialogues seem contradictory and disjointed because they reflect the dialogues' refutation of the idea of individuality as stable, private and set apart from its interactions with the public.

Wilde, in fact, argues that what gives each individual his uniqueness is the aspect of his personality which is being performed

4 Ibid., 215.

5 Ibid.

6 Herbert Sussman, 'Criticism as Art: Form in Oscar Wilde's Critical Writings,' *Studies in Philology* 70 (1973), 109.

7 Epifanio San Juan, Jr., *The Art of Oscar Wilde* (Princeton: Princeton University Press, 1967), 74.

at a given moment. He writes in 'The Decay of Lying' that 'what is interesting about people in good society . . . is the mask that each one of them wears, not the reality that lies behind the mask. It is a humiliating confession, but we are all of us made out of the same stuff.'[8] With this statement, Wilde declares the humanist argument that the internal self is the foundation of identity irrelevant. Instead, he sees individuality as constructed out of exhibition. The individual therefore cannot exist without being perceived by other people and these perceptions are always formed out of another's perceptual choices. One's sense of one's own identity then is inherently unstable because it is formed by so many different people privileging so many different (and sometimes contradictory) aspects. The essays reflect this phenomenon by replacing the stable, reliable authorial voice with a series of assertions and refutations.

'The Decay of Lying,' as an invective against the dictum 'truth in art,' is essentially Vivian's performance, with Cyril acting as the audience member attempting to integrate this new valuation of art into mainstream modes of thinking. Vivian in 'The Decay of Lying' puts forth the idea that we perceive our world through the tropes we encounter in art and literature. As an example, he suggests,

> The Nihilist, that strange martyr who has no faith, who goes to the stake without enthusiasm and dies for what he does not believe in, is a purely literary product. He was invented by Tourgénieff and completed by Dostoieffski. Robespierre came out of the pages of Rousseau as surely as the People's Palace rose out of the *débris* of a novel.[9]

The individuals, both general and specific, mentioned by Vivian in this passage are images of revolutionary figures, characterized by the public as representatives of certain political types. The real existence

8 Oscar Wilde, 'The Decay of Lying,' in *The Soul of Man under Socialism and Selected Critical Prose*, ed. Linda Dowling, 163–192 (London: Penguin, 2001), 169.

9 Ibid., 180–181.

of these figures is irrelevant; what matters, according to Wilde, is that literature has defined their images and we cannot conceive of revolutionaries without thinking of their literary counterparts. At one point in the essay, Cyril protests, 'But you don't mean to say that you seriously believe that Life imitates Art, that Life in fact is the mirror, and Art the reality?'[10] This objection prompts Vivian to launch into the main thesis of the essay, that art is the paradigm through which we perceive the world. Although Vivian is the primary performer in the essay, Cyril's gentle prodding serves both to enhance Vivian's performance and to underscore the vital role he plays in the development of Vivian's argument. Vivian may possess the same ideas without Cyril's presence but Cyril, by engaging with the ideas, enables Vivian to turn his theory into a dramatic performance.

For Wilde, there are two kinds of art: the artistic paradigm which shapes attitudes and responses and the particular visual, literary and performing arts which serve as manifestations of this paradigm. Both definitions of art give form and meaning to existence, as the artist becomes the architect of his or her way of being in the world. 'Art,' writes Wilde in 'The Decay of Lying,' 'is our spirited protest, our gallant attempt to teach Nature her proper place.'[11] Wilde believes that art creates its own meaning; rather than representing an external reality, it harbours within itself a reality which is, according to David Novitz, 'to be found in what is perceptible, tangible and wholly available to the senses.'[12] In the essay, Wilde notes the development of two distinct genres in nineteenth-century literary history, the fact-based works of Eliot's realism and Zola's naturalism and the more fantastical, self-consciously aesthetic works of Dante Gabriel Rossetti and William Morris. Whereas he disparages the former pair

10 Ibid., 179.

11 Ibid., 163.

12 David Novitz, 'Art, Life and Reality,' *British Journal of Aesthetics* 30, no. 4 (1990): 302.

of authors as being misguidedly didactic, he commends the latter because they convey that sense of wonder and delight that Wilde believes (as his short fiction especially demonstrates) gives pleasure to the reader and, through pleasure, understanding. The works of these aesthetic or fantastical writers are tantamount to a performance, where self-conscious artistry turns text into play and the reader into an imaginative co-creator of the text.

Wilde's defence of the romance, the fantasy, and even those realist works which he sees containing elements of the above may be symptomatic of his frustration with the way the press with its pretensions to factual writing continually misrepresented him. Certainly he was true to his argument in 'The Decay of Lying,' for none of his mature works can be classified as realism. His defence of these literary genres, however, is also illustrative of his argument that performance's meaning is neither direct nor didactic. It is subtle, it operates through the conveyance of pleasure rather than anxiety, and it often involves the appreciation of form, such as the essay itself being written as a dialogue rather than as a traditionally discursive argument.

In particular, Wilde's hostility to realism stems from the idea that the psychologically realistic novel, which aims to portray depth of character and of experience, in fact imposes a rigid model of behaviour onto its characters and a rigid style onto its authors. As Wilde mocks realist authors such as George Meredith and Mrs. Humphry Ward, he is mocking especially the idea of realism as a totalizing ideology. Characters' performances are limited to what is acceptable as mundane behaviour; they are not permitted to act in any way different from what is perceived as 'usual.' Differences are often seen as flaws, sometimes even tragic ones. Moreover the writing style suited to the realist novel is either overly subdued or didactic, attempting to educate the reader into the character's psychological complexities. But Wilde charges that these characters are not necessarily complex, only conforming to a literary style that purports to be truthful when, as he charges in 'The Decay of Lying,' it is merely another pose. He writes that if 'we regard Nature as the collection of phenomena external to man, people only discover in her what they bring to her. She has no suggestions of her own.'[13] The failure of realism, according to the essay, is that it does not allow room for the reader's interpretation. Instead, the reader is told how to understand the characters and even which reactions are appropriate.

Thus the liar becomes a heroic figure in the essay, the lone individual who realizes that the imagination is the key to the truth and who also understands that the imagination operates within the framework of art or artifice, rather than nature. Wilde writes:

> Art, breaking from the prison-house of realism, will run to greet [the liar], and will kiss his false beautiful lips, knowing that he alone is in possession of the great secret of all her manifestations, the secret that Truth is entirely and absolutely a matter of style.[14]

Wilde is not substituting a surface model with this statement. Style, to him, is the individual's performance; its purpose is to awaken an audience into contemplating the possible rather than the actual. The liar is so named not simply because he privileges imaginative possibilities over facts. He is a performer whose storytelling is that which is its own evidence. The liar is a self-contained text who escapes being a tautology by having meaning bound up in the pleasure and play of the story he tells.

Published in 1889, 'The Decay of Lying' is a prologue for the themes and concerns Wilde explores in his 1890 essay 'The Critic as Artist.' Whereas in 'The Decay of Lying,' the liar valiantly fights the tyranny of social conventions, in 'The Critic as Artist' the critic replaces the liar as the heroic figure. In 'The Critic as Artist,' Gilbert

---

13 Wilde, 'The Decay of Lying,' 173.

14 Ibid., 177.

argues that criticism allows the critic to make himself part of the work of art, projecting his own personality onto an existing work of art in order to create something altogether new. Through this argument, Gilbert critiques the work of Arnold and Ruskin who, in their endeavours to define and describe art, mandate a necessary distance between art and critic. The essay has greater affinities to Pater's work, certainly, but Wilde puts far more emphasis on the critic as the performer who embodies his critical views, giving his critic far more physical substance. In 'The Critic as Artist,' Gilbert states:

> That is what the highest Criticism really is, the record of one's own soul. It is more fascinating than history, as it is concerned simply with oneself. It is more delightful than philosophy, as its subject is concrete and not abstract, real and not vague. It is the only civilised form of autobiography, as it deals not with the events, but with the thoughts of one's life; not with life's physical accidents of deed and circumstance, but with the spiritual moods and imaginative passions of the mind.[15]

Criticism, as Gilbert describes it, fuses the individual's personality with the 'personality' one perceives in the work of art, creating a piece of writing which is imaginative rather than strictly expository. The aim of such criticism is to offer one a sense of the work of art as seen through the eyes of the critic, so that one never perceives the work of art independently from its criticism. One reads criticism therefore to gain an appreciation of the way art works upon its audience, or an appreciation of the relationship between art and audience. In this fashion, one can engage with criticism as if it too were a work of art, using one's own 'spiritual moods and imaginative passions' to create another work about the criticism as well as about the original work of art.

In contrast to Cyril's gentle prodding in 'The Decay of Lying,' Ernest in 'The Critic as Artist' takes on a more adversarial role. He

15 Wilde, 'The Critic as Artist,' 237.

argues overtly with Gilbert's statements, offering the conventional objections to Gilbert's novel ideas about criticism and the personality of the critic. In the essay, Ernest represents the individual schooled in classical aesthetics; his objections are conventional in that they follow the dicta about art set forth in classical texts. 'In the best days of art,' he states, 'there were no art-critics. The sculptor hewed from the marble block the great white-limbed Hermes that slept within it.'[16] Because Wilde seeks to ground his theories about art within the classical tradition, Ernest's ideas are extended rather than gainsaid throughout the essay. He may represent a conventional view about art, but it is not the view of the Philistine that needs to be dismissed. Rather, Gilbert uses these arguments to demonstrate how his new ideas evolve out of the classical traditions, bringing modern thought to the aesthetic concerns of the Ancient Greeks. Gilbert does not overturn Ernest's conventions, but calls for a return to older conventions, namely the classical privileging of sensation in the creation and criticism of art:

> It would be more just to say that the Greeks were a nation of art-critics . . . Recognising that the most perfect art is that which most fully mirrors man in all his infinite variety, they elaborated the criticism of language, considered in the light of the mere material of that art, to a point which we, with out accentual system of reasonable or emotional emphasis, can barely if at all attain.[17]

As Herbert Sussman notes, both the innovative and the conventional characters are 'masks for modes of thought attractive to Wilde.'[18] Cyril and Ernest represent the individual cultivated within the boundaries of social valuations; Vivian and Gilbert, through their refutation of conventional wisdom, represent the individual transcending or revaluing these boundaries. Lawrence Danson

16 Ibid., 218.
17 Ibid., 221–222.
18 Sussman, 'Criticism as Art,' 112.

points out that we find in the essays 'contradictions between a self-making and an always made self, a creative and created personality.'[19] Through their arguments, the two types of characters attempt to negotiate a space from which the individual can best perform. Both essays demonstrate a shift from Wilde's previous contention that the individual can use artistic forms to develop him- or herself more fully to a belief that the individual's own consciousness is constructed within the limitations of one's culture. 'Life holds the mirror up to Art,' he writes in 'The Decay of Lying,' 'and either reproduces some strange type imagined by painter or sculptor, or realises in fact what has been dreamed in fiction.'[20] Wilde believes that the personality of an individual is a construct that needs to be developed consciously in order for it to offer a critical counterpoint to common social practices. In 'The Critic as Artist' he writes, 'If you wish to understand others you must intensify your own individualism.'[21] The self here is potentially the repository for all knowledge but this knowledge remains dormant until it is put into use by everyday performance.

The question of performance in Wilde's essays relates directly to the problem of the modern subject in the nineteenth century. Specifically, the rise of scientific objectivism as well as the exaltation of industry and technology in the latter half of the century led to what many scholars have termed a crisis of the self in late-Victorian culture. In other words, as John A. Lester, Jr. explains it, one effect of scientific objectivism was to stress that objective reality eludes humankind. In particular, if the self can never be ascertained absolutely, then the subject loses its relationship to an external reality.[22]

19 Lawrence Danson, *Wilde's Intentions: The Artist in his Criticism* (Oxford: Clarendon, 1997), 18.
20 Wilde, 'The Decay of Lying,' 183.
21 Wilde, 'The Critic as Artist,' 245.
22 Lester, *Journey Through Despair*, 24.

As a reaction, the self becomes foregrounded as the only reality it is possible to know; by extension, then, the self becomes the only reality worth knowing. It is the signifier for the reality which escapes humankind's grasp. The self signifies all knowable reality by virtue of the fact that it is alienated from another reality. As Lester claims,

> What impinged on the literary mind of the [late Victorian] period was a disposition which . . . marks most existential thought, a resolve that, however bleak, hostile, or incomprehensible man's predicament is, nevertheless man must *be* and must find *significance in being*.[23]

Wilde uses the critic to argue that a person can shape the meaning of his world through the development and performance of his persona. 'The longer one studies life and literature,' he writes, 'the more strongly one feels that behind everything that is wonderful stands the individual, and that it is not the moment that makes the man, but the man who creates the age.'[24] The individual effects the same art that constructs him. He accomplishes this through art, of course, as he does in all of Wilde's previous writings about the individual; in 'The Critic as Artist,' however, Wilde, detailing his concepts of 'masks' and 'poses,' begins to examine this axiom. If the individual has the potential to present himself as a work of art and, in doing so, can alter the nature of his world, then what is involved and what is at stake in this process?

In 'The Critic as Artist,' Wilde imagines meaning as an energetic force, specifically the energy that is generated when one persona identifies with another persona. What makes this exchange of personae possible is the presence of desire or, more specifically, fascination. In 'The Decay of Lying,' Vivian's pronouncements are spurred on by Cyril's murmuring responses. Likewise, in 'The Critic as Artist,' Gilbert's arguments are furthered by either Ernest's as-

---

23 Ibid., 178.

24 Wilde, 'The Critic as Artist,' 228.

sents or by his misgivings; Ernest, by either agreeing or disagreeing, prompts Gilbert to extend his philosophizing. In 'The Soul of Man under Socialism,' Wilde presents the idea of a utopian state developing out of fascinating individuals and in 'Pen, Pencil and Poison,' he argues that the criminal Wainewright is fascinating enough that we cannot help but take pleasure in his misdeeds (an idea that is also the basis for *The Picture of Dorian Gray*). Fascination takes on an erotic quality in his essays in its transmission of both pleasure and enlightenment and it contributes to Wilde's conception of persona as a function of desire. In Wilde's essays, the fully-developed individual or personality exists because others find him compelling enough to want to interpret him.

The concept of fascination as an important element of a persona is Wilde's most transparent attempt to merge his intellectual theories with his daily life. Wilde had his first gay love affair with Robert Ross in 1886 and shortly afterwards began a series of short-lived liaisons with members of London's underground gay community. His fascination with several of these men found its way into his written works. In addition to inspiring fictional characters, the whole question of homoerotics alters his topics and writing style. The intellectually-based aesthetic pronouncements of the early 1880s begin to make way for the sensual, more decadent style of the 1890s. Lillie Langtry turns into Willie Hughes, in other words, and The New Helen into Dorian Gray and Salome.

Wilde was also sensitive to the idea of what is now called 'the closet,' and the masks and multiple personalities he describes have come to be associated with the idea of the double life a gay man in late-Victorian England was forced to perform. But masks are not only a sign of closeting to Wilde; artfully created, they can also be used to liberate the self. If one deliberately cultivates an artificial persona, then one can also pass an authentic self off as a mask. In other words, Wilde could 'play' gay, *be* gay, and have mainstream society think he was simply posing for effect. By turning identity into a playful double entendre, Wilde implicitly challenges the idea of an identity built upon normative practices. As Marvin Carlson notes, Wilde 'avoids claiming the stigma of homosexuality, but "manages" it by claiming an identity built upon . . . secondary signs' such as aestheticism or ornateness.[25]

Because of the double life he was leading, and also because of his frustration with the newspapers' narrow categorization of his persona in the 1880s, Wilde's idea of persona in his essays is one bounded only by the limitations found in artistic conventions. Disdaining the convention which privileges transparency in the individual, Wilde claims not only that the mask a person wears is the most interesting thing about him, but the mask is the thing that constructs the person. Wilde reiterates this belief in several places: in 'The Critic as Artist,' for instance, when he writes, 'Man is least himself when he talks in his own person. Give him a mask, and he will tell you the truth'[26] and in 'Pen, Pencil and Poison.' when he argues that Wainewright's pseudonyms, or authorial masks, 'intensified his personality.'[27] The mask, as a sign of concealment, paradoxically frees the individual to project a persona outside conventional norms. Since the concept of the self as stable and knowable in under question in the late nineteenth century, the mask, as the sign of a consciously-performed persona, passes for the knowable self in terms that an artistically-aware audience can appreciate.

The concept of the mask leads to Wilde's championing of the multiplicity inherent within the individual. Like the mask, multiple personae allow the individual to express attitudes and behaviours which resist cultural expectations. A writer could theoretically be both a hardworking husband and father and a member of homo-

---

25 Carlson, *Peformance*, 154.

26 Wilde, 'The Critic as Artist,' 261.

27 Oscar Wilde, 'Pen, Pencil and Poison,' in *The Soul of Man under Socialism and Selected Critical Prose*, ed. Linda Dowling, 193–212 (London: Penguin, 2001), 195.

sexual circles. He could both court and mock the press and mainstream publicity. He could speak in a number of disparate voices and have them all come together under the authorial name 'Oscar Wilde.' If a single self is allowed only one course of experience, a personality which is multiple can take advantage of contradictions and paradoxes in life in order to experience it more fully.

A persona's ability to fascinate needs the presence of another in order to bring it to full fruition. Wilde writes, 'If you wish to understand others you must intensify your own individualism.'[28] One must also perform one's individualism for others to form impressions of it. Wilde's critic is therefore his vision of the ideal audience for a persona. The critic, according to Wilde, is an avid reader of the persona of a work of art, whether human or inanimate. He interprets the art he encounters through an exchange between the persona of the work of art and the persona he cultivates within himself. Wilde writes that

> the critic will be an interpreter, if he chooses. He can pass from his synthetic impression of the work of art as a whole, to an analysis or exposition of the work itself . . . Yet his object will not always be to explain the work of art. He may seek rather to deepen its mystery, to raise round it, and round its maker, the mist of wonder which is dear to both gods and worshippers alike.[29]

The critic receives his impressions from both the textual meaning of the work of art and the intertextual references contained within its meaning. He then integrates the work of art into his own persona, performing the impressions he has received from previous encounters with art in order to create a text for others to continue the critical process. Thus, according to Wilde,

---

28 Wilde, 'The Critic as Artist,' 245.

29 Ibid., 244.

> it is only by intensifying his own personality that the critic can interpret the personality and work of others, and the more strongly this personality enters into the interpretation, the more real the interpretation becomes, the more satisfying, the more convincing, and the more true.[30]

Wilde takes as an example the famous nineteenth-century pianist Anton Rubinstein. He claims:

> When Rubinstein plays to us the *Sonata Appassionata* of Beethoven he gives us not merely Beethoven, but also himself, and so gives us Beethoven absolutely – Beethoven reinterpreted through a rich artistic nature, and made vivid and wonderful to us by a new and intense personality.[31]

The original work by Beethoven becomes indistinguishable from Rubinstein's Beethoven; the audience's knowledge of the *Appassionata* is altered by its impression of Beethoven's music as interpreted by Rubinstein. According to Wilde, this new version of Beethoven is a combination of the original piece, Rubinstein's interpretation and each audience member's individual personality, which reconstructs the experience out of his or her impressions about the performance. In this vein, Rubinstein's performance becomes multiplied as each audience member forms an individualized interpretation of the sonata according to his or her personality. 'There are as many Hamlets as there are melancholies,' he writes in 'The Critic as Artist;'[32] later, in a letter arguing for the literary merit of *The Picture of Dorian Gray*, he writes, 'What Dorian's sins are no one knows. He who finds them has brought them.'[33]

'The Portrait of Mr. W.H.' marks the culmination of Wilde's initial theory of performance and persona before his later works begin to complicate it; indeed it is the only one of his critical writings

30 Ibid., 245.

31 Ibid., 246.

32 Ibid.

33 Wilde, *Complete Letters*, 439.

that directly incorporates performance and the theatre into his arguments. Persona, performance and the pursuit of art deftly interweave to show how the fascination with an individual's persona can be used as a critical tool. In this hybrid of essay and story describing a fictional attempt to prove that the 'W.H.' to whom Shakespeare dedicated his sonnets was a charismatic Elizabethan boy actor, Wilde argues that the interpretation of the sonnets rests on appreciating and, to a large degree, absorbing the persona of Willie Hughes. The fact, however, that Willie Hughes is ultimately a cipher, or a false centre, reveals the irony behind the fascinating persona. What really impels the interpretation in this essay, according to Wilde, is the persona that each critic creates for himself and displaces onto this fictional character named Willie Hughes. It is the epitome of performance in criticism, using Willie Hughes as a mask for the critic and thereby aestheticizing the criticism and presenting it as an art form independent of Shakespeare's sonnets.

In 'The Portrait of Mr. W.H.,' Wilde extends the conceit of the muse that he first employed in his poems about Sarah Bernhardt and Lillie Langtry. Wilde uses the figure of Hughes in an attempt to, as John Lester puts it, 'shun all absolutes, to view the true nature of things as being unknowable, and then, wilfully and knowingly, find or fabricate illusions and *believe* in them.'[34] It is an act of play on Wilde's part, a desire to let the imagination construct its own truth unhampered by realistic conventions or claims to historical accuracy. The liar in 'The Decay of Lying' becomes in a sense the author of 'The Portrait of Mr. W.H.,' aiming to prove that truth in interpretation is imaginative, dependent on the force of one's ability to realize one's fantasies.

'The Portrait of Mr. W.H.''s unusual provenance points to the influence that Wilde's Willie Hughes exerted on the London artistic community. Wilde wrote two versions of 'Mr. W.H.': a shorter version which was published in *Blackwood's Edinburgh Magazine* in

34 Lester, *Journey Through Despair*, 177.

July 1889, and an expanded version which he hoped to publish as a book. Wilde struck a tentative publication deal with Charles Ricketts, and Ricketts painted a 'portrait' of Willie Hughes which was to be the frontispiece of the books. Ricketts' imaginary portrait evokes the text of 'Mr. W.H.'; it is his vision of the fake Clouet portrait that represents, for both the narrator and for Erskine, the concept of truth as an imaginative creation. A fictional portrait referencing a forged portrait also echoes the essay's challenge to the concept of truth in interpretation. Ricketts' portrait might be an imaginative recreation but, according to Wilde, it is not more so than any other attempt to reconstruct the past. Unlike historical research, however, the imaginative recreation of Willie Hughes adds an extra element by using Hughes as a gateway to understanding Shakespeare. The persona collectively embodied by Shakespeare's sonnets is given form and meaning by the fictional Willie Hughes. To Wilde, a fictionalized forged portrait interprets the essence of the sonnets in a much more convincing way than the 'factual' scholarship mocked in this essay.

Moreover, Ricketts' portrait acts as a tangible sign for the fictional portrait of Willie Hughes. Wilde managed to convince A.J. Balfour of Willie Hughes' existence, for example, and the American playwright Clyde Fitch sent Wilde the following letter:

> *I* believe in Willie Hughes: I don't care if the whole thing is out of your amazing beautiful brain. I don't care for the laughter, I only know I *am* convinced and I *will.*
>
> I will believe in Willie H.
>
> Sometime, if the Gods are kind I shall *send you* a picture of Mr . W.H., it may be another forgery. – But that won't make any difference, will it?[35]

35 Letter, Clyde Fitch to Oscar Wilde [1889?]. Oscar Wilde and His Literary Circle. William Andrews Clark Memorial Library, University of California, Los Angeles.

Willie Hughes briefly became a code for homosexual love, like the green carnations worn in the lapels of the New Hedonists. It is appropriate that 'Mr. W.H.' and its theme of inspiration and muses deals almost openly with the erotic attraction between men, as its writing coincides with Wilde's immersion in London's gay subculture. Whereas his previous essays were concerned with the importance of fascination and attraction in abstract terms, 'Mr. W.H.' shows explicitly how fascination constructs a persona out of the acts and gestures of another individual. Furthermore, 'Mr. W.H.' demonstrates that the fascination one man has for another can transcend the interpretive level and actuate artistic creation.

The narrative of 'Mr. W.H.' unfolds in a series of frames: the core narrative, about the research conducted to confirm the existence of Willie Hughes, is framed by several stories of erotic attachment: the alleged attraction of Shakespeare to Willie Hughes, and the real attractions of Erskine to Cyril and of the narrator to Erskine. In addition, the essay is further enfolded in a meta-frame of Wilde's own romances. 'Mr. W.H.''s unfolding love stories reflect Wilde's fascination with his lovers and the realization that his relationship with these young men (or the acknowledgment of his homosexuality) could lead him to expand both his persona and his creativity beyond his previous limits.

Each of the love stories in 'Mr. W.H.' ends with the lovers unfulfilled. This sense of aborted romance not only permeates 'Mr. W.H.' but becomes the point from which the exchange of personae develops. The difficulties experienced by the lovers can be described using Slavoj Žižek's terms 'the problem of "the fulfillment of desire,"' a series of displacement which occurs as one searches for a never-attainable real object. Žižek, following Lacan, writes that

> when we encounter in reality an object which has all the properties of the fantasized object of desire, we are nevertheless necessarily somewhat disappointed; we experience a certain 'this is not it;' it becomes evident that the

finally found real object is not the reference of desire even though it possesses all the required properties.[36]

In 'Mr. W.H.,' fascination with an individual is an expression of the desire to find fulfillment in the real. The unconscious realization that the real cannot be attained, especially not within another person, leads to the eventual dissolution of the relationship. The exchange of personae provides a way to both approximate the fulfillment impossible to achieve in the relationship itself and retain a trace of the relationship after it has foundered. Thus the essay's characters, none of them able to acknowledge openly their erotic attraction, cathect their desires onto the story of Willie Hughes.

Wilde addresses the problem of the fulfillment of desire by having each of his characters use Willie Hughes as the representation of their respective desires. Willie Hughes' persona in effect is constructed by each character's projection of his desire. Cyril, an amateur actor who once excelled in the female roles played by the Elizabethan boy actors, emphasizes a Willie Hughes 'who was a really vital factor in the development of [Shakespeare's] dramatic art.'[37] Erskine's fascination with Willie Hughes grows out of his fascination with Cyril; he sublimates his desire for Cyril onto his interest in Shakespeare's love for Hughes. Playing on the mirroring relationships, Erskine's point of entry into the Willie Hughes theory is his discovery of the puns on Hughes' name supposedly present in the sonnets. Indeed, Cyril's presentation of a forged portrait to Erskine is his attempt to make real *both* relationships. The portrait, however, like the unspoken love between Cyril and Erskine, is put under question. As an appeal to the 'laws' of portraiture, which hold that the subject portrayed be a real person, the portrait fails. Likewise, Cyril and Erskine can never display their attraction according

36 Slavoj Žižek, *The Sublime Object of Ideology* (London: Verso, 1989), 91.
37 Wilde, 'The Portrait of Mr. W.H.,' 38.

to the laws of a socially-legitimate love relationship. Both the portrait and the hope of an open romantic relationship, then, become ideals impossible to attain. Their 'forgeries' therefore become displaced performances of unfulfilled desire, substitutions that engage, as Judith Butler writes, 'a fantasy of recovering a primary object of a love lost – and produced – through prohibition.'[38]

For the narrator, who is intrigued by both Erskine and by his recollections of Cyril, Willie Hughes becomes the nexus of fascination itself. The narrator claims that 'Willie Hughes became to me a kind of spiritual presence, an ever-dominating personality.'[39] Willie Hughes becomes to the narrator the sign of both Cyril's love of the performing arts and Erskine's desire for Cyril. The narrator's Willie Hughes is both the protean boy actor and the elusive love object. As a result, this Willie Hughes synthesizes the desire of Cyril and Erskine. Wilde writes, '"How is it," says Shakespeare to Willie Hughes, "that you have so many personalities?" and then he goes on to point out that his beauty is such that it "seems to realise every form and phase of fancy, to embody each dream of the creative imagination."'[40] Willie Hughes' personalities are constructed by his various audiences: the audience that sees him perform, the playwright who is inspired by him, and the amateur performers centuries later who seek to reconstruct him out of their own desires.

In putting emphasis on the role of the other in the construction of persona, 'Mr. W.H.' returns to Wilde's insistence that presenting one's persona is an act of performance. Like Wilde's use of the Lillie Langtry persona, the performance involves creating a character and using it as an imaginary reference for the self. Žižek points out that every identification is a twofold process. One identifies with an

38 Judith Butler, *Bodies That Matter: On the Discursive Limits of 'Sex'* (New York: Routledge, 1993), 99.

39 Wilde, 'The Portrait of Mr. W.H.,' 58.

40 Ibid., 50.

image representing 'what we would like to be.' In this act of imaginary identification, we also identify with 'the very place *from where* we look at ourselves so that we appear to ourselves likeable, worth of love.'[41] In short, the character one creates, or the front one uses as an artistic mask, represents both an idealized version of the self and the position from where the conditions of this idealization arise. But the performance of the self is only realized completely when it is reflected back onto the self by the appreciation of another. This strategy therefore implicates everyone involved in the individual's performance. For Wilde, the self's performance opens up a community of personae, each persona building on the performance of other individuals to create a world based on art.

Thus 'Mr. W.H.' is preoccupied as much with the nature of performing as it is with fascination. Here, theatrical performance becomes a metaphor for art and all the erotic desire it contains. '[A]ll art,' Wilde writes, '[is] to a certain degree a mode of acting, an attempt to realise one's own personality on some imaginative plane out of reach of the trammelling accidents and limitations of real life.'[42] The masks and multiple personalities to which Wilde refers in 'The Critic as Artist' find their fullest expression in 'Mr. W.H.,' especially in the portrayal of Cyril as a modern-day boy actor. Wilde was interested in the idea of actors cross-dressing in their roles; while editing *The Woman's World*, he published an article by Lady Archibald Campbell about her pastoral Shakespeare productions, featuring engraved illustrations of Ellen Terry as Orlando in *As You Like It*. As well, the idea of gender as a malleable performance is an extension of his work with the androgynous-looking Lillie Langtry in the early 1880s. In 'Mr. W.H.,' he writes, 'Of all the motives of dramatic curiosity used by our great playwrights, there is none more

41 Žižek, *The Sublime Object of Ideology*, 105.

42 Wilde, 'The Portrait of Mr. W.H.,' 33.

subtle or more fascinating than the ambiguity of the sexes.'[43] For Wilde, the ability of a male actor to project a feminine persona epitomizes his belief that performance can successfully subvert the codes of behaviour dictated by social conventions. Moreover, switching gender personae exemplifies the concept of the artistically-created self; one can perform a persona that runs counter to one's gendered body and can do so by creating a persona which treats gender as an imaginary rather than biological state.

For Wilde, what makes the performance of the boy actor compelling is the interplay of mimetic performance and gender obfuscation. By maintaining a physical distance from his role, the boy actor encourages his audience to avoid a literal interpretation of his performance. As Wilde writes:

> To say that only a woman can portray the passions of a woman, and that therefore no boy can play Rosalind, is to rob the art of acting of all claim to objectivity, and to assign to the mere accident of sex what properly belongs to imaginative insight and creative energy.[44]

Wilde looks to the stage as a model for the conscious creation of a self and sees the stage as the one place where this imaginative transformation can occur without corruption or compromise. And, more importantly, Wilde keeps returning to the idea of the stage as a safe space from which to play with the attributes society holds to be immutable. He reasons that if he can convince his readers to turn all the world into a stage, then every aspect of life could be as safe a performing space as the theatre. Thus there would be no deviance, only performances. Subversion would be labelled as art and socially-marginalized behaviour would be seen as an element of a persona demanding to be appreciated, rather than censured, for its differences.

---

43 Ibid., 72.

44 Ibid., 73.

'The Soul of Man under Socialism' is Wilde's imagining of the interpersonal exchange of personae as a paradigm for social reform. The essay was written out of Wilde's brief attendance at the Fabian Society meetings in 1888, where he was introduced to the group's socialist platforms. In the essay, Wilde argues that a society operating by means of the exchange of personae could potentially transform itself into a utopian state.

For Wilde, art in 'The Soul of Man' is the fully-developed persona, one which exists as a direct refutation to social norms. 'Most personalities,' he writes, 'have been obliged to be rebels. Half their strength has been wasted in friction.'[45] Wilde believes that the reliance on the working class for manual labour stultifies the working class' potential as citizens; moreover, the middle and upper classes' reliance on the workers also limits their own development of their personalities by forcing upon them the roles of exploiters, the only part they are allowed to play. 'An enormously wealthy merchant,' Wilde claims, 'may be – often is – at every moment of his life at the mercy of things that are not under his control.'[46] Wilde envisions a society under socialism which would replace a market based on the exchange of labour with one based on the exchange of art. The more artistically-developed the individual, the more compelling the persona, the greater an individual's capital would be.

At the heart of Wilde's argument in 'The Soul of Man' is a disdainful look at commodity culture. Even though Wilde participated in the marketing of his own image, he knew all too well the distortions on his persona imposed by a market seeking to turn him into a stereotype. As Carolyn Lesjak suggests:

> Wilde's decadence and aestheticism, his self-generation of the personality 'Oscar Wilde,' his multiple posturings, sexual practices, and epigrammatic

45 Oscar Wilde, 'The Soul of Man under Socialism,' in *The Soul of Man under Socialism*, ed. Linda Dowling, 125–160 (London: Penguin, 2001), 134.

46 Ibid., 133.

style of mimicry and reversal can be seen as interventions into the increasingly limited and limiting public sphere of late-Victorian capitalist culture.[47]

To Wilde, the development of personae is valuable as a foundation for culture precisely because, although it can be commodified, its meaning constantly eludes the market's attempts to label it. Since a persona comes into being because of a connection made between two people and more importantly since the character of each persona takes shape out of desire, at the heart of any individual's persona is a transgressive desire, one which exists against the conforming impulses of mainstream society.

Despite his insistence that the individual with a fully-developed persona could flourish outside of commodity culture, Wilde, by describing persona as an intersection between self and other, still has persona influenced by the commodity culture he is also wary of. What he argues for in this essay, though, is awareness of one's persona and the conscious work needed towards developing it. By doing so, the individual can use the strategies of commodity culture in order to transcend it. Wilde insists at first that the value of a persona lies in its uniqueness and that each singular person develops an aura which marks it as a work of art. Unlike Walter Benjamin's concept of the aura, a persona is constantly being recontextualized as it relies on the impression of another to give it form. Like Benjamin's concept of the commodity, however, a persona is the sum of a series of fragments; Wilde's idea of multiple personalities suggests that the idea of the integrated persona is a fiction perpetuated for its simplicity. Wilde is not contradicting himself here; rather, he is in fact attempting to synthesize art and commodity into the persona, which would ultimately have value but would be outside the control of the marketplace.

---

47 Carolyn Lesjak, 'Utopia, Use, and the Everyday: Oscar Wilde and a New Economy of Pleasure,' *ELH* 67, no. 1 (2000), 181.

Wilde, as Paul A. Cantor suggests, 'finds the very notion of a market economy repellent, especially when it draws art into its orbit and turns the work of art into a commodity that can be bought and sold at prices set by the public.'[48] The arguments in 'The Soul of Man' not only reflect his own struggle with the press over his persona, but also look towards the idea of revisioning society as communitas, representing, as Turner describes it,

> the desire for a total, unmediated relationship between person and person, a relationship which nevertheless does not submerge one in the other but safeguards their uniqueness in the very act of realizing their commonness.[49]

For Wilde, a fully-developed persona is the result of personal bonds having been formed, whether through admiration, friendship or eroticism, which could feasibly weaken the class system – valuing an individual because of the persona he or she cultivates is a rejection of hegemonic stereotyping. Christ becomes the socialist artist in this essay because of his cultivation of individuality in himself and in others, thereby imagining an existence for his followers free of Roman hierarchies. Therefore Wilde can offer a vision of a collective utopian state that uses individualism as its motivating force.

Wilde in 'The Soul of Man' sees the marketplace as a symptom of social control. By encouraging his readers to use their personae to subvert the market, he is also urging them to fight other social pressures as well. Individualism to Wilde is 'a disturbing and disintegrating force. Therein lies its immense value. For what it seeks to disturb is monotony of type, slavery of custom, tyranny of habit, and the reduction of man to the level of machine.'[50] Like 'The

---

48 Paul A. Cantor, 'Oscar Wilde: The Man of Soul Under Socialism,' in *Beauty and the Critic: Aesthetics in an Age of Cultural Studies*, ed. James Sonderholm, 74–93 (Tuscaloosa, AL: University of Alabama Press, 1997), 84.

49 Turner, *Dramas, Fields, and Metaphors*, 274.

50 Wilde, 'The Soul of Man under Socialism,' 144.

Decay of Lying,' 'The Soul of Man' recognizes that society has the power to condition behaviours and responses and in both essays Wilde proclaims the necessity of using persona as a defence of one's individuality in the face of social controls. But as Wilde envisions a society based upon the free exchange of personae, he implicitly wonders whether an individual's relationship to his society prohibits a utopian state from ever being realized.

In his series of essays, Wilde transforms his idea of persona, changing it from an exaltation of the performing individual to a complex theory based upon interpersonal exchanges to a suggestion about its potentially revolutionary qualities. The concept of persona becomes a critical tool in these essays, one which liberates the self to experience life outside of Victorian conventionality. Yet the relationship between self and society remains problematic in these essays as Wilde tries to find a way to have the artistically-developed self interact with social strictures without having everything end in tragedy. In 'The Soul of Man,' his solution is to imagine a world not yet possible in order to warn his reader of the pressures of the society in which they live. While writing his essays, Wilde was also working on *The Picture of Dorian Gray*; shortly after completing these texts, he wrote *Salome*. It is in these two works that Wilde explores his anxiety over the limits of persona that he hinted at in his essays. The fear that the notion of persona as a means of exchange is fundamentally unstable and might not hold up against the tyranny of Victorian norms becomes a large part of the thematic structures of both *Dorian Gray* and *Salome*. Although these essays suggest that performing one's persona in all of its different aspects opens up possibilities for alternative modes of conduct, Wilde's work on performance and persona is far from complete. The next period in his literary activity explores a darker side of persona and an attempt to reconcile the performing individual with the social conventions against which he or she struggles.

Chapter Four
Decadent Anxiety and Negative Capabilities: *The Picture of Dorian Gray* and *Salome*

Wilde's two major works of 1890 and 1891, *The Picture of Dorian Gray* and *Salome*, complicate the ideas about persona he put forth in his essays. The two works are essentially variations on the same theme, one which introduces a sombre note into his theories of persona and performance. Wilde's essays are for the most part positivist in nature, where he sees the development of a persona as a mark of aesthetic progress in late-Victorian culture. His articulations of fascination and desire in essays like 'The Critic as Artist' and 'The Portrait of Mr. W.H.' affirm the potential a developed persona has to spur both intellectual thought and art. But both *The Picture of Dorian Gray* and *Salome* turn away from the idea of positive development of one's persona, seeing it instead as a means for misdirection, corruption, and ultimately self-destruction. Rather than focusing on an active performance, the attention Wilde pays to the more static persona serves to reinforce his criticisms about his culture's misguided tendency towards using a persona as a fixed, non-changeable type. A persona, as an image constructed out of desire, is a powerful and often chaotic force – if taken out of the hands of its subject, it has the potential to destroy rather than create.

Rather than being a carefully-constructed artificial image, a persona in these works is a barely-contained evocation of Schopenhauer's Will, made fascinating to us because of our identification with the incessant desiring of the Will. For all his paradoxes and subversive reversals, Wilde was serious about the idea that cultivating a persona can profoundly impact one's culture. He also believed that, because of its importance to both identity and culture, a persona needs to be constructed according to a series of ethical laws, laws in which the public should be educated. *Dorian Gray* and *Salome* are cautionary tales detailing what might happen should these ethics be ignored.

Wilde furthers the connection between desire and persona he established in 'The Portrait of Mr. W.H.' in these two 'decadent' works of the early 1890s, but he subverts the connection here in order to present the antithesis to his performance theory. In *Dorian Gray* and *Salome*, Wilde alleges that aestheticism, by focusing on the individual as a beautiful object rather than as a subjective being, prevents rather than facilitates one from incorporating one's desires into one's persona. The result, he claims, is a perverted persona intent on destroying the existing beauty in the world. For Wilde, as Richard Ellmann, notes, 'aestheticism was not a creed but a problem. Exploring its ramifications provided him with his subject.'[1] Even though Wilde began his career as an aesthete, in these works he realizes that aestheticism, while allowing individuals to transcend the Philistine aspects of their society, also limits the experiences available to them. In particular, aestheticism runs the risk of robbing sexual desire of its power by attempting to transform all experiences into contemplative acts. The question remains: if everything is contemplation, where then is the outlet for such a powerful force as desire? In *Dorian Gray* and *Salome*, the protagonists are trapped within aestheticized personae. Because they can only function as objects of desire, there is no psychological space for them to develop subjective desire. Wilde here is constructing a proto-Freudian argument that the repressed's only recourse is to break through the pressure of the ego and either force its way into consciousness or reveal itself through action.[2] The resulting action invariably throws

1 Ellmann, *Oscar Wilde*, 310.

2 Sigmund Freud, *Beyond the Pleasure Principle*, ed. and trans. James Strachey (New York: Norton, 1961), 20.

out of balance the ego's role of stabilizing the individual; thus, the individual's desire becomes perverted.

The question of sexual desire and its relationship to one's persona even appears in the publication history of the novel. In *The Picture of Dorian Gray*, Wilde brought the corruption of the London sexual underworld into the London drawing-room in order to show that the perversion of a persona is a common problem, or at least a problem that transcends class. Despite the presence noted by several critics of homosexual desire in the novel, however, Wilde's early drafts of *Dorian Gray* demonstrate a continuing effort to subsume the discourse of homosexuality into a discourse of persona. Donald Lawler argues that the 'so-called purging of the novel' of overt gay references 'was not an attempt to placate critics but rather part of a plan of revision conceived by the author after the first draft of his novel has been written and long before the story appeared in print.'[3] Lawler's study of the early holograph and typescript of the novel reveals that although J.M. Stoddart, the editor at *Lippincott's Monthly Magazine* where the 1890 novella version of *Dorian Gray* was published, did delete some of the more explicit homoerotic phrases, Wilde was responsible for 'aestheticizing' most of the homoeroticism in the novel and that he did so of his own volition.

By changing the relationships between Basil, Henry and Dorian from ones based on erotic desire to ones based on art, *Dorian Gray* articulates Wilde's theories of persona and performance through a more vaguely realized discourse of homosexual desire. Jeffrey Nunokawa points out that Wilde was anxious about writing a novel that dealt explicitly with homosexual desire, remarking that though this desire 'spills out into the wider boulevards of the novel's plot

3 Donald Lawler, 'The Revisions of *Dorian Gray*.' *Victorian Institutes Journal* 3 (1974), 21. Lawler also notes that Wilde revised *Dorian Gray* at least three times before it was published in *Lippincott's Monthly Magazine* in 1890.

and takes the prouder place of explicit topic,'[4] it disappears into heterosexual marriage (Dorian's brief engagement to Sibyl), morbidity (Basil's death), or an acknowledgment that it was no more than a youthful folly (Dorian's later courtship of Hetty Merton).[5] Wilde was aware that the mere mention of homosexuality would foreclose any ideas he put forth. However, he was also aware that the foundations of a persona – fascination and desire – were, as he conceived it, heavily rooted in both a homosexual tradition and, to him, best revealed in contemporary times through the particular intellectual and erotic attachments between men. For Wilde, as Ellmann points out, the notion of either idealized love or passion never extended to relations between men and women.[6]

By the time he was writing *Dorian Gray*, Wilde had been sexually involved with younger, attractive men such as Robert Ross, the poets John Gray and Lionel Johnson, and several working-class youths. The erotic fascination these men held for him was reciprocated by his charismatic performance when he told stories or carried a conversation. (Indeed, many of his friends and former lovers speak of Wilde's gifts as a *raconteur.*) Moreover, during this period Wilde's interest in decadent literature grew. Marc-André Raffalovich recalled discussing Rachilde's *Monsieur Vénus* with Wilde and that Wilde enjoyed the novel so much he was shocked to hear that the author was only twenty years old.[7] Rachilde's novel, about a woman who takes a male lover as her mistress, deriving sexual pleasure in dominating him as a man would ordinarily dominate his

4 Jeffrey Nunokawa, 'The Disappearance of the Homosexual in *The Picture of Dorian Gray*,' in *Professions of Desire: Lesbian and Gay Studies in Literature*, ed. George E. Haggerty and Bonnie Zimmerman, 183–190 (New York: Modern Language Association, 1995), 183.

5 Jeffrey Nunokawa, 'Oscar Wilde in Japan: Aestheticism, Orientalism, and the Derealization of the Homosexual.' *Positions* 2, no. 1 (1994), 44.

6 Ellmann, *Oscar Wilde*, 283–284.

7 Ibid., 282.

kept woman, has as one of its themes the multiplicity inherent in sexuality. Sexuality in *Monsieur Vénus* is constructed along the same lines as a persona: sexual experiences can be used to cultivate one's persona as much as artistic experiences can. Yet although *Dorian Gray* shares this theme with *Monsieur Vénus*, it is not nearly as explicit in its articulation. Wilde's ambitions for the novel were for mainstream publication and general acceptance, his decadence one that could interest rather than alienate the general reading public.

Wilde's anxiety about the homosexual desire present in *Dorian Gray* is perhaps best expressed in the following passage, removed by him from the original manuscript: 'But the world might guess it; where there is love, they would see something evil. Where there is spiritual passion, they would suggest something vile.'[8] In his revisions, Wilde systematically excised the more concrete representations of homosexual desire. The revisions of the original manuscript to the 1890 version of the story published in *Lippincott's* constitute one set of excisions; more dramatic revisions were made for the novelization of the story in response to newspaper reviewers' criticisms of the story's erotic content. Again, Wilde had to contend with the press' blunt attempt to categorize his work (this time as effeminate and immoral) but he also had to deal with the material cosnequences of the reviews and articles. W.H. Smith, at the time the largest retailer of books and magazines in Britain, pulled copies of *Lippincott's* from its racks[9] after one review in the *Scots Observer*, typical of the 1890 reviews in the type of censure it employs, stated that if Wilde 'can write for none but outlawed noblemen and perverted telegraph-boys, the sooner he

8 Oscar Wilde, *The Picture of Dorian Gray*, 1890 and 1891 ed., ed. Donald L. Lawler (New York: Norton, 1988), 181. Unless otherwise indicated, references to *Dorian Gray* will be to the 1891 full-length novel.

9 Joseph Bristow, 'Wilde, *Dorian Gray*, and Gross Indecency,' in *Sexual Sameness: Textual Differences in Lesbian and Gay Writing*, ed. Joseph Bristow, 44–63 (London and New York: Routledge, 1992), 52.

takes to tailoring (or some other decent trade) the better for his own reputations and the public morals.'[10]

The most significant revision from the magazine story to the novel is the characterization of Basil Hallward's attachment to Dorian. The passages Wilde removed from the magazine story alter Basil's attitude from a romantic attachment to a more generalized attitude of reverence of an artist towards his subject. Rather than having Basil's art subsume his sexuality altogether, Wilde makes his sexuality an integral part of his artistic temperament. Wilde wrote the following paragraph in the 1890 magazine story where Basil describes his feelings towards Dorian:

> 'Then why won't you exhibit his portrait?' [asked Lord Henry].
>
> 'Because I have put into it all the extraordinary romance of which, of course, I have never *dared* to speak to him. He knows nothing about it. He will never know anything about it.'[11]

In 1891, Wilde revised the passage:

> 'Then why won't you exhibit his portrait?' asked Lord Henry.
>
> 'Because, without intending it, I have put into it some expression of all this curious artistic idolatry, of which, of course, I have never *cared* to speak to him. He knows nothing about it. He shall never know anything about it.'[12] [emphasis in both passages mine]

In the 1891 version, not only does Basil describe his feelings for Dorian as an effect of an artist's technical and formal fascination

---

10 'Reviews and Magazines,' *Scots Observer*, 5 July 1890. The phrase 'outlawed noblemen and perverted telegraph-boys' is a reference to the 1889 Cleveland Street Scandal, in which members of England's aristocracy were discovered to be clients of a London gay brothel.

11 Wilde, *The Picture of Dorian Gray*, 1890 ed., 181.

12 Wilde, *The Picture of Dorian Gray*, 15.

with a beautiful subject, he also disavows the erotic aspects of his fascination with Dorian. The erotic feelings in the 1890 version are transformed into a more abstract artistic appreciation.

Although Wilde changes specific homoerotic desires in the novel to a more abstract fascination with Dorian's image, he still connects the construction of a persona to unspoken desire. Dorian's persona, that of the beautiful innocent protégé portrayed in Ancient Greece, of which his first name serves as a constant reminder, is desired as art. *Dorian Gray* is a novel in which persona is used as a means of misdirection, revealing its artistic origins by concealing its roots in homosexual desire. Dorian is, as Ed Cohen argues, an image created out of Basil and Henry's competing desires for him.[13] However, by the final edition of the story, these desires have become grounded firmly in aesthetics rather than erotics. Basil's fascination with Dorian in the 1891 edition rests on his belief that painting Dorian will turn him into a better artist and the strong physical attraction Basil has for Dorian is relegated to the margins of the text. Because a persona by its nature is an act of misdirection, focusing attention only on selected aspects of the self, in *Dorian Gray* it also serves as a metaphor for the textualization of homosexual desire. Homosexual desire may serve as a fundamental discourse of the novel but persona supplies the language through which this discourse is articulated.

What happens in the novel is that although the homosexual eventually 'disappears,' as Nunokawa argues, Dorian's persona proliferates. Dorian circulates throughout the novel by means of other characters' responses to him. For Basil, 'a curious sensation of terror' comes over him upon meeting Dorian for the first time. He tells Henry, 'I knew that I had come face to face with some one whose mere personality was so fascinating that, if I allowed it to do

13 Ed Cohen, 'Writing Gone Wilde: Homoerotic Desire in the Closet of Representation,' *PMLA* 102, no. 5 (1987), 806.

so, it would absorb my whole nature, my whole soul, my very art itself.'[14] Sibyl Vane's girlish construction of Dorian arises from her 'call[ing] on Memory to remake him [as Prince Charming].'[15] To Alan Campbell, 'as to many others, Dorian Gray was the type of everything that is wonderful and fascinating in life.'[16] Even Henry, upon hearing about Dorian's parentage, remarks that '[i]t posed the lad, made him more perfect as it were.'[17] Dorian's persona is given substance in the novel by other characters' specific approaches to him, whether it be Sibyl's naive romanticism, Henry's desire for influence, or Basil's erotically-coded aestheticism. By using Dorian as a blank canvas, so to speak, Wilde exemplifies one of the fundamental principles of persona he put forth in his essays, that exposure to a fascinating persona causes one to develop one's own personality. Dorian apparently makes Basil a better artist, Henry a sharper observer of human nature, Alan more hedonistic, and Sibyl more of a helpless, passive romantic heroine, and he manages to do so simply by displaying his persona and letting his audience interpret it.

The Picture of Dorian Gray is Wilde's adaptation of the Faust legend as a cynical look at late Victorian culture, where the pursuit of beauty and youth have replaced Marlowe's Faustus' and Goethe's Faust's hunger for alchemical knowledge. One of the problems the novel brings to light is that beauty, and particularly the persona of the young and beautiful boy, has become interchangeable with knowledge, even though, as Wilde writes in 'The Critic as Artist,' 'Beauty reveals everything, because it expresses nothing.' [18] Throughout his essays, Wilde presents an idea of beauty as something which refracts meaning, a hermeneutic tool which in and of

14 Wilde, *The Picture of Dorian Gray*, 11.

15 Ibid., 52.

16 Ibid., 129.

17 Ibid., 33.

18 Wilde, 'The Critic as Artist,' 240.

itself signifies nothing because it has no need to. In the novel, Lord Henry, the Mephistophelian character in the novel, presents youth and beauty as a form of alchemy, the mode through which every experience and therefore every access to knowledge is available and transmutable. In the novel, Wilde does not refute this assertion but argues that beauty, like knowledge, is a terrible form of power, one which constantly escapes the individual trying to control it.

The vexed relationships between beauty, art, and knowledge run throughout the novel. In *Dorian Gray*, Wilde describes a society in which the cultivation and performance of a persona is the primary vehicle through which one engages in interpersonal relationships and understands one's relationship to the world. The problem in the novel is that a persona is appreciated by the novel's characters *only* as art, without any concession to the dynamics instrumental in its development, especially those emanating from one's desires. Wilde cautions that a human being, no matter how beautiful, is not art. His or her ability to change, to grow, and to develop is likely the human faculty which Wilde prizes the most and which is at the root of his writings about performance. Even a stone statue like the Happy Prince or an aged cantankerous Selfish Giant is redeemed because of his capacity for change. So when a dynamic persona and a static work of art become interchangeable, whether in the case of Dorian and his portrait or in the case of other characters treating Dorian as if he were art, the self's identity becomes bounded by the parameters of art; art, as Kathryn Humphreys puts it, becomes 'a substitute for character itself.'[19] It is no accident that the seeds of Dorian's corruption are planted the moment he sees the finished portrait: 'A look of joy came into his eyes, as if he had recognized himself for the first time. . . . The sense of his own beauty came on him like a

19 Kathryn Humphreys, 'The Artistic Exchange: *Dorian Gray* at the *Sacred Fount.*' *Texas Studies in Literature and Language* 32, no. 4 (1990), 524.

revelation. He had never felt it before.'[20] The portrait arouses Dorian's desire and stifles it at the same time by denying Dorian an independent subjectivity.

In *Dorian Gray*, a persona's apparently seamless facade conceals a personality which is actually fragmented and dissociated. Dorian's portrait is a clear example: Dorian perceives the portrait as a series of separate images (a cunning look, a bloodstained hand), each bearing less and less resemblance to his own image. The image of the 'real' Dorian, as represented by the picture, can only be glimpsed in parts, its hideousness increasingly distanced from the image of the public Dorian. Sibyl Vane becomes the novel's most telling example of the impossibility of uniting a persona in the novel. Dorian's doomed affair with her is analogous to the Gretchen tragedy in Goethe's *Faust*. As a character, Sibyl is constructed out of the performances she gives and Dorian's infatuation with her increases the more she seems to embody the various roles that she plays. He blatantly acknowledges that he has fallen in love with Rosalind and Juliet and Imogen, fascinated by Sibyl's ability to switch personalities and even gender performance at will. To Dorian, Sibyl is a prism of personalities – not a single woman, but one who promises a multitude of experiences with a multiplicity of theatrical female characters. She ceases to be an object of desire when she can no longer multiply her personae. And, in turn, Dorian cannot respond to Sibyl as a single individual; she becomes to him a 'third-rate actress with a pretty face.' [21]

Sibyl is too innocent to take pleasure in her various performances. She clings to a romantic, conventional notion of love, one which holds that authentic love prohibits the need for performance. In a comedy, Sibyl might be gently persuaded to embrace her multiple roles or persuade Dorian to abandon his need for them; in

---

20 Wilde, *The Picture of Dorian Gray*, 25.

21 Ibid., 70.

Dorian Gray, this misunderstanding kills her. Sibyl, however, is also the vehicle through which Dorian begins to multiply his own personalities. Her suicide is what causes the picture to begin its change and it is notable that, even though Dorian did not murder her with his own hands, his influence and subsequent rejection is what leads her to her death. It is a reversal of Wilde's argument in 'The Portrait of Mr.W.H.' – here, influence does not develop Sibyl's persona, it destroys her instead.

Through Basil and Henry, the novel explores a dialectic between a positivist view of persona and a decadent one. Basil believes that the surface image is a transparent manifestation of the inner self. He not only believes that beauty is synonymous with goodness, but that a persona based on physical beauty can strengthen the aesthetics of anyone coming into contact with this persona. As Basil explains his secret to his recent artistic success:

> It is one of the best things I have ever done. And why is it so? Because, while I was painting it, Dorian Gray sat beside me. Some subtle influence passed from him to me, and for the first time in my life I saw in the plain woodland the wonder I had always looked for, and always missed.[22]

For Basil (with a covert nod to Ruskin), persona means progress; its influence improves his work, advances his contribution to art, and therefore becomes an indication of a higher moral order.

Henry, on the other hand, believes, as Sheldon W. Liebman explains:

> that there is no moral order (the universe is purposeless and indifferent to human needs); that the self is not only multiple, but at war with itself and driven by forces beyond its control, and that morality is arbitrary and relative.[23]

---

22 Ibid., 14.

23 Sheldon W. Liebman, 'Character Design in *The Picture of Dorian Gray*.' *Studies in the Novel* 31, no. 3 (1999), 297–98.

A persona, according to Henry, conceals this divided self, gathering the fragments of a disjoined, multiple inner self into a mask, projecting an illusion of a coherent self while secretly celebrating its inner disjuncture. Henry's philosophy of hedonism neatly fragments the body itself into different personae:

> The body sins once, and has done with its sin, for action is a mode of purification. Nothing remains then but the recollection of a pleasure, or the luxury of a regret. The only way to get rid of a temptation is to yield to it. Resist it, and your soul grows sick with longing for the things it has forbidden to itself, with desire for what its monstrous laws have made monstrous and unlawful. It has been said that the great events of the world take place in the brain. It is in the brain, and the brain only, that the great sins of the world take place also.[24]

To Henry, the purpose of cultivating the self is the pleasure the self can take from this process. Influence, especially the artistic influence to which Basil refers, is the means to experience new sensations. And this pleasure is an end in itself since, for Henry, there is no point in appealing to a system of values outside the self's own bodily sensations. A persona, to Henry (and with his covert nod to Schopenhauer), reveals that humans are animalistic beings, intent on the gratification of these senses. All appeals to a higher good external to the self are nothing more than a rationalization in order to justify humanity's beastly nature.

With their respective philosophies, Henry and Basil offer competing views on treating an individual's persona as a work of art. Dorian's persona is the model that structures their opinions; Dorian is regarded as a work of art because his persona lends itself to different interpretations of his inner character. Indeed, since Dorian's own opinions seem to develop from Basil and Henry, he can never exert his own will in a manner independent of the beliefs of his two

24 Wilde, *The Picture of Dorian Gray*, 20.

mentors. Dorian himself is an empty signifier. Like a work of art, his significance depends entirely on the perceptions of his interpreters. To Basil, Dorian cannot be distinguished from his portrait. Because Dorian merely reflects, Basil believes that he has no personal agency and can thus conclude that Dorian's beauty renders him an innocent. To Henry, though, Dorian represents the work of art as commodity. Henry's repeated exhortations to Dorian to experiment with his senses, to derive pleasure through his youth and beauty and to exhibit himself to the public whenever possible is a thinly-veiled urging for Dorian to offer himself both socially and sexually for public consumption. As a result, Henry's relationship to Dorian, despite his teachings, is that of a purveyor of art rather than a creator. Basil may get artistic satisfaction from having secured Dorian in the world of art, but Henry's satisfaction comes from seeing Dorian circulate among the upper classes.

It is through Henry's relationship with Dorian that Wilde's narrative turns darkly ironic. The transition Dorian makes from Basil's innocent passive muse to Henry's decadent protégé marks, according to Wilde, a noticeable deterioration in his status as art. Indeed, the more Dorian indulges in corrupt behaviour, the less Dorian exudes an image of purity and disinterestedness representative of Basil's aesthetic ideals. In actuality, according to the definition put forth by Mark Sagoff, Dorian exhibits more of the qualities pertaining to a forgery than to a genuine work of art:

> While minute, yet important, differences may be assumed to exist between the originals and reproductions, these differences are likely to favour the copy. The reason is the one we noted: old paintings deteriorate; a forgery,

> therefore, may look more like the original looked at its creation than the original now resembles its former self.[25]

With Sagoff's definition, Dorian's authenticity becomes reversed – it is the *painting* that is deemed the original work of art, echoed by Basil's wistful comment that the picture is the 'real' Dorian, and Dorian himself who is the copy. Accordingly, the original is locked away, accessible to almost no one, while the copy circulates among the public. Indeed, part of Dorian's corruption is that he circulates too much. Instead of remaining the social darling of the upper classes, he crosses class lines too freely and mixes classes to suit his whims. As Dorian defensively snaps at Basil,

> You ask me about Henry Ashton and young Perth. Did I teach the one his vices, and the other his debauchery? If Kent's silly son takes his wife from the streets, what is that to me? If Adrian Singleton writes his friend's name across a bill, am I his keeper?[26]

Dorian's corruption is evidenced in the novel not by any of his actions, which with the exception of Basil's murder remain deliberately vague in the narrative, but by his threat to the integrity of the upper classes. Like a forgery which is passed off as a genuine work of art, Dorian subverts the exclusivity of his class and therefore endangers its integrity.

The transformation of Dorian from art to forgery suggests that both art and persona, if left unchecked, can deteriorate into noise. As Henry tells Dorian, 'To me, Beauty is the wonder of wonders. It is only shallow people who do not judge by appearances. The true mystery of the world is the visible, not the invisible.'[27] But Dorian

25 Mark Sagoff, 'On the Aesthetic and Economic Value of Art,' in *Aesthetics*, ed. Susan Feagin and Patrick Maynard, 119–128 (Oxford and New York: Oxford University Press, 1997), 124.

26 Wilde, *The Picture of Dorian Gray*, 118.

27 Ibid., 23.

fundamentally misunderstands Henry's poetic musings about art. To Henry, and to Basil to a lesser degree, art is essentially abstract, something that can exist only as an intellectual function. Henry lives by that creed, talking about art's potential to influence behaviour but never attempting to put his theories into practice. As Basil chides him in one instance, 'You never say a moral thing, and you never do a wrong thing. Your cynicism is simply a pose.'[28] Dorian, however, interprets Henry's words literally and this is where he makes his error. Henry's statements are contemplative exercises; as such, they do not work in practice. Dorian tries to refute the belief that art stands apart from everyday practices by trying to make his own desires art. Human beings, because of their dynamic nature, cannot become art, and Dorian's attempt violates the principles of both art and humanity, hence his inability to keep his persona cohesive or his actions good.

Wilde's statement in 'The Critic as Artist' that an individual should construct himself as a work of art seems to fall apart as Dorian's behaviour becomes more and more destructive throughout the course of the novel. Wilde implies in the novel, however, that the problem with Dorian's actions is not necessarily that he is trying to live his life through art, but that he has a narrow comprehension of what art is. He sees art and sensual gratification as interchangeable, betraying Basil's belief in art as a sanctified relationship between two people and even Henry's belief that the pursuit of new pleasures and experiences are separate from the sphere of art. Dorian's interpretation is based largely on his own vanity rather than on an intellectual consideration of the nature of art and his vanity inevitably leads to narcissism. The only person to whom Dorian seeks to give pleasure is himself. The more intent he becomes on developing his persona, the more he shuts himself away from the world. Dorian's failing is that he is unable to use his per-

28 Ibid., 10.

sona to form relationships with others, a negation of Wilde's belief that persona is at the centre of interpersonal exchanges. In the beginning of the novel, he merely reflects both Basil and Henry's ideas about beauty; as he grows increasingly corrupt, his short-lived friendships and romances only serve to feed his own sensations. As Elaine Smith notes, 'Dorian Gray, for all his dalliances, leads a life devoid of true friendship and understanding. In his search for tactile sensations, he destroys anyone – male or female – who attempts emotional closeness.'[29] If Dorian is supposed to be the leader of Henry's 'new Hedonism,' he fails, because he is unable to amass any followers. And the reason he has no followers is that the only disciple he truly is interested in courting is himself.

Dorian's failure is largely due to his misapplication of the aesthetic lifestyle. Rather than having art enable his humanity, he uses art to replace it. Art signifies perfection in the novel only because it at the same time represents immobility and stagnation, qualities antithetical to the human experience. In order to become a work of art, Dorian essentially has to deny his own humanity which includes a sense of accountability to a higher moral order. Dorian, upon realizing that the portrait manifests the signs of his interior life, comes to the conclusion that, like a work of art, he is immune to change, presumably immune to death, and thus free to act without any fear of retribution in this world or the next:

> For there would be a real pleasure in watching [the picture change]. He would be able to follow his mind into its secret places. This portrait would be to him the most magical of mirrors. As it had revealed to him his own body, so it would reveal to him his own soul. And when winter came upon it, he would still be standing where spring trembles on the verge of summer. When the blood crept from its face, and left behind a pallid mask of chalk with

---

29 Elaine Smith, 'Oscar Wilde's *The Picture of Dorian Gray*: A Decadent Portrait of Life in Art – or Art in Life.' *Publications of the Arkansas Philological Association* 19, no. 1 (1993), 24.

> leaden eyes, he would keep the glamour of boyhood. Not one blossom of his loveliness would ever fade. Not one pulse of his life would ever weaken. Like the gods of the Greeks, he would be strong, and fleet, and joyous. What did it matter what happened to the coloured image on the canvas? He would be safe. That was everything.[30]

The realization that the portrait will absorb both the effects of time and the consequences of his sins liberates Dorian to become the living work of art – a thing of beauty and fascination, perhaps, but also a thing living outside the social and moral codes of everyday life. The thrill Dorian receives from seeing the picture change is a narcissistic one. Not only does his own body become a work of art but he is also free from the need to form those relationships that will help him develop his persona. Moreover, Dorian's epiphany lays bare the separation of one's public persona and one's interior life. With the threat to his beauty, as well as the threat of death and final judgment removed, Dorian no longer needs to foster a relationship with the world.

So Dorian retreats, like Huysmans' Des Esseintes, into his own aestheticized space and spends years studying such inanimate artifacts as jewels and textiles. Everything that Dorian looks at becomes another mirror in which he can admire his own reflection; his famous yellow book, for example, 'seemed to him to contain the story of his own life, written before he had lived it.'[31] His objects of study are meant for his own gratification and also as a displacement for his own latent feelings of guilt and unease; they are 'to be to him means of forgetfulness. Modes by which he could escape, for a season, from

30 Wilde, *The Picture of Dorian Gray*, 84.

31 Ibid., 99. In Wilde's 1890 typescript, the yellow book was named *Le Secret de Raoul* and attributed to the fictional author Catulle Sarrazin. Wilde originally connected the yellow book to Dorian's corruption more explicitly. See Wilde, *The Picture of Dorian Gray*, 1890 ed., 240*n*.

the fear that seemed to him at times almost too great to be borne.'[32] As the portrait becomes more and more grotesque (and less like his reflection), he turns to embroideries, perfumes and stones for identification. However, these objects, as Dorian reads them, are merely signs of the historical decadent figures portrayed in the yellow book. In order to integrate them fully into his own persona, Dorian begins to perform these historical figures publicly, cross-dressing like Anne de Joyeuse and engaging in debauched behaviour like Pietro Riario. Significantly, men who murdered the women they loved, such as the Duke of Milan and Malatesta, fascinate Dorian. He uses these legends as a means of forgetting Sibyl Vane and by rationalizing his repressed guilt by 'look[ing] on evil simply as a mode through which he could realize his conception of the beautiful.'[33] Like the material goods he is obsessed with, these historical figures serve to adorn his persona by misdirecting the audience. Dorian uses his youth and beauty, as well as his increased sophistication, to tacitly refute accusations of his corruption. Even as several members of society shun him, artists such as Basil and women such as the Duchess of Monmouth still cannot look beyond his image.

The relationship between Dorian and his portrait and the consequential narcissism that Dorian exhibits illustrates Wilde's anxiety about the limits of persona. For Wilde, a persona can be a form of performance or a form of visual art, but either requires an interplay with an audience in order for a persona to be fully realized. Turning away from another human being, even if one turns towards works of art instead, can result in the disintegration of the persona. In Dorian's case, he shows signs of ennui even before his death. 'I wish I could love,' he complains to Henry, '[b]ut I seem to have lost the passion, and forgotten the desire. I am too much concentrated on myself. My own personality has become a burden to me. I want to escape, to go

32 Ibid., 109.

33 Ibid., 115.

away, to forget.'[34] A persona, according to Wilde, is always created out of change, whether as the result of an exchange between individuals or as the result of an ongoing process of development. It is an art of a kinetic type. Thus in order to develop, a persona must refer constantly to things outside of itself. In Dorian's case, when his persona refers only to his portrait – as the beautiful work of art with no soul – he cannot develop. He can only deteriorate.

Although Wilde repeatedly implies that Dorian needs to be accountable to some higher moral order, he also stresses repeatedly that *fin-de-siècle* society is the last place in which this moral order can be found. Attempts to thwart Dorian are consistently unsuccessful: Basil's efforts to convince Dorian of his wrongdoing end in his murder, Alan Campbell's feeble protests end in his suicide and, most notably, James Vane's attempts to avenge his sister's death end in his own accidental death. Furthermore, despite the rumours of Dorian's corrupting influence, he continues to be sought after for society teas and dinners. Indeed, those rumours which cause Basil such distress seem to be hardly noticed by the society doyennes who beg for Dorian's company. Lady Narborough sums up her set's regard for Dorian when she tells him, '[Y]ou are made to be good – you look so good.'[35] Even within society's fashionable circles, Dorian's role is mostly to be an object of beauty; most of the repartee at the social gatherings involves Henry, with Dorian sitting quietly to one side. The upper classes, Wilde implies, enable Dorian's corruption because they treat him as a consumable object.

Wilde's anxiety about persona manifests itself in *The Picture of Dorian Gray* through the image of the beautiful boy who misunderstands his own role in aesthetic culture. As he writes in the Preface to the novel, 'All art is at once surface and symbol. Those who go beneath the surface do so at their peril. Those who read the symbol

34 Ibid., 156.

35 Ibid., 138.

do so at their peril.'[36] The novel is in a sense a horror story about the consequences which befall a Philistine culture that wilfully misreads persona. For Wilde, the proper appreciation of a persona can potentially make the difference between living in a culture based upon art or a culture based upon the repression of art. Failing to treat a persona as a synthesis of art and the individual will not make art disappear, but it will pervert it, turning the beautiful boy into a moral grotesque.

Although Wilde began writing *Salome* in 1891, he had toyed with the idea of contributing to the body of nineteenth-century literature on the Biblical figure for some time prior to beginning the play. Wilde was familiar with the narrative iconography that had sprung up around Salome in the decades prior to his drama, from Flaubert's 'Hérodias' to Mallarmé's unfinished poem 'Hérodiade' to Gustave Moreau's paintings of Salome immortalized by J.K. Huysmans in *A Rebours*, to name a few. Wilde, however, planned to distinguish his portrayal of Salome from those of the writers and painters before him; he found, for example, previous depictions of the princess by artists such as Leonardo da Vinci and Albrecht Dürer unsatisfactory. The Salome of Wilde's drama differs also from her previous literary incarnations. In Flaubert's story, for instance, Herodias is the instigator of both Salome's dance and request for John the Baptist's head. Salome is a pawn in this case in Herodias' struggle for power with Herod. Wilde, by giving Salome her own motive for dancing before Herod, returns to the princess a measure of subjectivity that had been denied her ever since the Bible omitted her name from its tales of John's beheading.

Of all the previous depictions of Salome, the paintings by Moreau and especially Huysmans's description of them influenced Wilde the most in his conception of the princess. According to Richard Ellmann, Wilde liked to recite the passages in *A Rebours*

36 Ibid., 3.

about the Moreau paintings.[37] From the beginning, Wilde conceived of Salome as an icon. He saw Salome as the representation of all the unspoken impulses and desires he had written about in *The Picture of Dorian Gray*. Yet Wilde takes his character of Salome further than he does Dorian. Not only does his Salome articulate the motivations that are kept concealed in *Dorian Gray*, but Wilde gives her a justification for her actions that he deliberately keeps ambiguous with Dorian.

Indeed, Wilde attributes to Salome a great deal more subjectivity than Dorian. Originally, Wilde intended to call his drama *The Decapitation of Salome* and planned to have Salome become a saint at the end of the play.[38] Although he abandoned that idea in favour of exploiting the legend of Salome as a *femme fatale*, vestiges of the more hagiographic version remain in the play. Wilde's Salome is an attempt to combine her iconic reputation with a more psychologically-based portrait. It is sometimes an uneasy mix in the play; the aesthetic discourse and intoning language of the play divert from Salome's character and encourage the audience to look at her only as an image rather than as a motivated character. John Paul Riquelme, representing the views of several critics, argues, 'Any interpretation that understands Salomé's language as realistic, that is, as a transparent vehicle for rendering the thoughts of a psychologically believable character, presents a distorted view of the play.'[39] Such a view overlooks the point Wilde is making in the play about the dangers involved in treating Salome exclusively as an image. While Riquelme is right in cautioning against looking at Salome as a realistic discourse, he dismisses the possibility that Wilde is juxtaposing psychological realism with aesthetic discourse. The reason behind this odd com-

37 Ellmann, *Oscar Wilde*, 342.

38 Ibid., 344.

39 J.P. Riquelme, 'Shalom/Solomon/*Salomé*: Modernism and Wilde's Aesthetic Politics.' *Centennial Review* 39, no. 3 (1995), 582.

bination is Wilde's argument that by privileging the effects of language over its content, the audience commits the same errors against Salome that the other characters in the play do, appreciating her image at the expense of her subjectivity. Thus, in examining the consequences of such a view, Wilde includes the audience as being complicit in the fundamental problem of the play by overlooking the anger and destructiveness inherent in Salome's persona.

For *Salome* in effect extends and complicates the argument Wilde puts forth in *Dorian Gray*, namely that when control over a persona is taken away from the individual, the individual's desires will threaten to pervert his or her persona. Moreover, *Salome* shows, as *Dorian Gray* did previously, that through the misreading of a persona, an individual can assume a sort of illicit power which threatens the established order of things. *Salome* in fact blatantly expresses the will, desire and quest for power that *Dorian Gray* leaves ambiguous; as Christopher Nassaar notes, 'Salome sheds Dorian's inhibitions and emerges as an unrestrained sexual murderess.'[40]

The character of Salome suggests that a persona has a greater importance for the female performer. As a dancer and object of desire, Salome is, as several scholars have noted, particularly susceptible to the male gaze. Furthermore, her status as a woman who can perform implies that her persona is vulnerable to chameleon-like change. Wilde had hoped that Sarah Bernhardt would perform the role. As Riquelme points out, casting the middle-aged Bernhardt as Salome would have discouraged the audience from interpreting the play realistically.[41] Presumably, as the audience looks at Salome, they would see not only Wilde's character, but the Salomes of past writers and artists, as well as Bernhardt's persona. Wilde's Salome is trapped within her own persona as the epitome of the *femme fatale* and his

40 Christopher Nassaar, 'Wilde's *The Picture of Dorian Gray* and *Salome*.' *Explicator* 57, no.1 (1988), 35.

41 Riquelme, 'Shalom/Solomon/*Salomé*,' 583.

play, rather than being a literal retelling of the Biblical story, becomes an exploration of the limits of persona and of its symbolic value.

In *Salome,* the moon serves as a metaphor for the empty canvas and for Salome herself. Like Dorian Gray, the moon assumes whatever significance the viewer attaches to it. In the play, the moon is a 'dead woman' according to Herodias's Page,[42] a 'princess' according to the Syrian Narraboth,[43] a 'mad woman' according to Herod,[44] and 'money' and a 'virgin' according to Salome herself.[45] These descriptions of the moon reveal the different watchers' desires for Salome, up to a point. More specifically, however, the descriptions point to the way their desires construct their respective states of mind. For instance, the 'dead woman' of the Page's vision can be attributed partially to his jealousy of Narraboth's erotic attraction to Salome. Herod's image of the moon as a 'mad woman' is based upon his uncontrollable desire for Salome. Indeed, his lust for her will eventually cause him to make the mad gesture of offering her whatever she wants provided she satisfies his desire. In light of Herod's perspective, Salome's view of the moon as both 'money' and a 'virgin' points to her awareness that her body, at least as far as Herod is concerned, has an exchangeable value.

Interestingly, the only figure who sees nothing in the moon but its own image is Herodias, who snaps at Herod that 'the moon is like the moon.'[46] By virtue of her refusal to interpret the moon, Herodias displays her unwillingness to acknowledge her daughter's importance to these men and this is underscored by her repeated admonitions to Herod not to look at Salome.[47] (It is worth noting that

42 Oscar Wilde, *Salome*, in *The Importance of Being Earnest and Other Plays*, ed. Peter Raby, 61–91 (Oxford: Oxford University Press, 2008), 65.

43 Ibid.

44 Ibid., 75.

45 Ibid., 68.

46 Ibid., 75.

47 Ibid., 76–77.

the Page is also upset when his loved one, Narraboth, 'looks too much' upon Salome.)[48] Salome poses a distinct threat to Herodias. As Herod has a history of taking the women he likes to look upon, the possibility exists for Salome to usurp her mother's throne. For Herodias, then, Salome possesses a power through her desirability that has the potential to destroy Herodias's position. Salome's connection to the moon, then, threatens to destabilize the power held by the one other woman in the court. Because of this, she is estranged from her mother.

Thus Salome is set up from the beginning as being a woman whose persona is a figure of iconic beauty and an object of sexual desire, and not much else. The danger in this, according to Wilde, is that Salome indeed has a will and desires of her own, but because of her position in the play has no outlet to express them. Hanna B. Lewis notes that 'Salomé is presented as a "fait accompli"'[49] and the reason for this is that the characters in the play have conspired to keep Salome from expressing her subjectivity; as an object of the gaze, Salome is kept inanimate and stagnant. But Salome's status as an object is misleading. Since she cannot exert her own power in creating her own persona, her frustration and resentment cause her to seek other avenues of power.

Because of the emphasis Wilde places upon the act of looking, the play in large part attempts to negotiate between the dangers of looking too much and the dangers of not looking enough. As Brad Bucknell notes, 'There is almost no one in the play who is not involved in some kind of projection, some kind of complex interplay between the eye and the object of vision.'[50] This interplay takes the form of a narcissistic relationship with the self, in that the object of

48 Ibid., 65.

49 Hanna B. Lewis, 'Salome and Elektra: Sisters or Strangers.' *Orbis Litterarum* 31 (1976), 129.

50 Brad Bucknell, 'On "Seeing" Salome.' *ELH* 60, no. 2 (1993), 515.

vision, Salome, invariably takes the form of the viewer's desires. An excess of looking, therefore, leads to destruction, as evidenced by both Narraboth's suicide and Herod's reluctant murder of Jokanaan.

Looking at Salome for any length of time leads to the consumption of the self by its own desire. Salome, for instance, compels Narraboth to do her bidding with the promise of a future look and Narraboth commits suicide because of his inability to cope with Salome looking at someone else. Looking at Salome is an attempt to own Salome, to turn her into the Salome each one who looks at her wants her to be. Salome's persona is therefore malleable; the image she projects shifts according to the desires of those who encounter her. The mistake the characters make regarding her persona is in thinking that Salome, because she does not look at herself, can claim no ownership over her own persona. This is the same moral theme that Wilde used in *Dorian Gray* – like Dorian, Salome's awareness of the effect her own persona has on other characters leads her to wield a certain power over their perceptions. But Salome's relationship to her own persona is refracted through the perceptions of the other characters. Since she is seen as an object of desire, she can only act out of desire, alienated from any moral or even rational judgment on her part that might mitigate her choices.

Of course, the only character who steadfastly refuses to look at Salome is Jokanaan. Critics have long described Jokanaan as an oral rather than a visual character and this is true to a great extent, but Jokanaan is more image-sensitive than they have given him credit for being. Jokanaan speaks in images; his prophecies of the coming of Christ are evocative word-paintings. 'The son of man is at hand,' he intones. 'The centaurs have hidden themselves in the rivers, and the sirens have left the rivers, and are lying beneath the leaves of the forest.'[51] More importantly, as Jokanaan is forced to engage with

51 Wilde, *Salome*, 68.

Herod's court, his language becomes even more descriptive. He cries about Herodias:

> Where is she who gave herself unto the Captains of Assyria, who have baldricks on their loins, and tiaras of divers colours on their heads? Where is she who hath given herself to the young men of Egypt, who are clothed in fine linen and purple, whose shields are of gold, whose helmets are of silver, whose bodies are mighty?[52]

Jokanaan's aesthetic prose ties him to the men of Herod's court, particularly Herod himself and, to a lesser degree, the Page. He speaks about Herodias in terms of commodities, categorizing her and by extension Salome as the sum of her material goods. This is where Jokanaan errs with respect to Salome and where precisely he makes the same mistake as Herod: by being unable to see Salome as anything other than a materialist creature, he dismisses the passion and the rage underlying Salome's actions and therefore underestimates her reaction to him.

For the one thing that characterizes Salome above all else is her resentment against being limited by her visuality, particularly when this visuality fragments her into fetishized parts. Herod, the man who desires Salome, is fixated upon her mouth; to him, it is a symbol of sexual orality, and Herod heightens his desire of Salome by both infantilizing her and linking her mouth directly to intoxicating wine and fertile fruit. Herod says to Salome about the wine, 'Dip into it thy little red lips, that I may drain the cup'[53] and when he asks her to ear some fruit, he says, 'I love to see in a fruit the mark of thy little teeth. Bite but a little of this fruit and then I will eat what is left.'[54] With these requests, Herod makes clear that Salome is an object of desire that he, as a king, has the power to consume sexually

52 Ibid., 71.
53 Ibid., 76.
54 Ibid., 77.

by literally consuming the fruit and wine bearing the mark of Salome's fetishized mouth. When Salome resists Herod's advances by maintaining that she is neither thirsty nor hungry, Herod petulantly turns against her mother and offers Salome Herodias' throne to sit on. His implication is that if Salome allows her beauty to be exploited, she can achieve the power of a queen. However, the power that Herod offers Salome is qualified, since she can only flourish by being bounded by the parameters of his desire for her. Moreover, Herod makes it plain by focusing exclusively on her sexualized parts that his desire dismisses Salome as a subjective entity. By treating Salome as an object, Herod neglects the fact that Salome too can see, can desire, and can use the power she possesses as princess of the court to further her own ends.

When Salome focuses her desire on Jokanaan, she pointedly appropriates Herod's seductive discourse, as if by doing so she can appropriate his power. Like Herod's fixation on her mouth and teeth, Salome's desire for Jokanaan takes the form of ever-increasing synecdoche, first concentrating on his body, then his hair, then his mouth. Salome also speaks in the aesthetic discourse used by the men in the play: 'Thy hair is like the cedars of Lebanon . . . that give their shade to the lions and to the robbers who would hide themselves by day.'[55] Salome purposefully ignores what Jokanaan is saying in order that she may look at him. Like Herod, Salome overlooks Jokanaan's subjectivity in favour of an appreciation of his body, an aggressive move that she is clearly not that comfortable with, since she appears to be unsure of what tack she should take in her attempt at seduction. Jokanaan's body, to Salome, is 'white like the lilies of the field,'[56] then it is 'like a leper' and 'like a whitened sepulchre full of loathsome things,'[57] moving from an image of

55 Ibid., 73.

56 Ibid., 72.

57 Ibid., 73.

fertility to an image of decay. His hair is first 'like clusters of grapes,'[58] but Salome changes this description to 'a crown of thorns which they have placed on thy forehead' and 'a knot of black serpents writhing around thy neck.'[59] In her attempted seduction, Salome draws her imagery from Jokanaan's Biblical story. The leper is Lazarus, raised by Christ from the dead. The 'whitened sepulchre' is a reference to Christ's criticism of the Jewish practice of painting tombs white in order to purify them. Christ chastises the Jews for this practice because the coat of paint provides only a superficial veneer of cleanliness. He rebukes the Jewish elders by claiming that they 'are like whitewashed tombs which on the outside appear beautiful, but inside they are full of dead men's bones and all uncleanness.'[60] With this allusion, Salome turns the words of Christ back onto Jokanaan. She focuses not only on his surface qualities but implicitly accuses him of believing that her surface beauty necessarily conceals a degenerated interior.

Salome's description of Jokanaan's hair contains, besides the reference to Christ's crown of thorns worn at the Crucifixion, another allusion to the Biblical story of John the Baptist. Jokanaan, in the Gospel according to St. Matthew, is preaching in the wilderness of Judea, clad, as the First Soldier in Salome reiterates, in 'camel's hair, and round his loins he had a leathern belt.'[61] The 'knot of vipers' refers to the epithet hurled by Jokanaan at the Pharisees and Saduccees, who insincerely request to be baptized.[62] In Salome's

58 Ibid.

59 Ibid.

60 Matthew 23:27.

61 Wilde, *Salome.*, 67. See Matthew 3:4: 'Now John himself had a garment of camel's hair, and a leather belt about his waist; and the food was locusts and wild honey.' The First Soldier's description of Jokanaan has him coming '[f]rom the desert, where he fed on locusts and wild honey. He was clothed in camel's hair, and round his loins he had a leathern belt.'

62 Matthew 3:7.

description, however, the vipers are crawling around Jokanaan's neck, threatening to strangle him. Salome mocks Jokanaan for his intolerance; the infidels that he sought to bar from God's grace literally return to kill him.

When Salome shifts her gaze to Jokanaan's mouth, the instrument for both his prophecies and his censures, she has no need to draw a Biblical analogy. Salome's images of Jokanaan's mouth are a mix of sensuality – she compares his mouth to pomegranates and precious stones – and, when she compares his mouth to the blast of military trumpets and the feet of a hunter, violence. As an object of sexual desire in Herod's court, Salome is well aware that passion is fraught with danger, and Wilde also uses the combination to point out that every passion contains within it its own potential for destruction. More importantly, though, as Eibhar Walshe notes, 'Salomé offends against a traditional system of male desire by articulating her own, independent desire for the body of the Prophet.'[63] As Salome becomes more passionate, she also becomes more subversive, and her power over her own image (as the subject rather than the object of desire) palpably grows until Herod quashes it with his fetishizing gaze.

When Salome uses Biblical analogies to describe Jokanaan's physical attributes, she returns Jokanaan's perception of her because, as Martine Thomas points out, Salome and Jokanaan 'are unable to hear the meaning of their mutual words, since they only feel the resistance their words imply.'[64] Salome uses Jokanaan's reputation in order to construct her perception of him. Whereas Jokanaan reviles Salome based on his preconceptions of her as her mother's daughter, Salome uses established preconceptions of Jo-

63 Eibhar Walshe, '"Angels of Death": Wilde's Salome and Shaw's Saint Joan.' *Irish University Review* 27, no.1 (1997), 31.

64 Martine Thomas, 'Oscar Wilde's *Salome*: A Few "Fin de Siecle" Aspects.' *Cahiers victoriens et edouardiens* 36 (1992), 157.

kanaan to fuel her attraction to him. Unlike Jokanaan's treatment of her, Salome refuses to dismiss him on account of his image as an infidel-hating ascetic. Salome sees in her fixation on Jokanaan's image a way to attain the power denied her as a perpetual object. She too can manipulate perceptions in order to get the object of her desire and, significantly, she can do so with a man outside of Herod's court hierarchy. Salome's attempted seduction of Jokanaan is an attempt to find power outside the court and particularly to find a form of subjective power, one in which her power is not dependent on the gazes of others.

Salome and Jokanaan thus relate to each other from their own isolated perceptions. Elliott L. Gilbert notes that the play is 'a veritable taxonomy of solipsism.'[65] Just as Salome is trapped within her visualization of Jokanaan, Jokanaan is likewise circumscribed by how he sees the princess. When he looks at Salome, he can only see Herodias. When Salome introduces herself to him, Jokanaan responds by crying out, 'Back! Daughter of Babylon!' and continues, 'Thy mother hath filled the earth with the wine of her iniquities, and the cry of her sins hath come up to the ears of God.'[66] Jokanaan refuses to look at Salome because he has already seen her before. Salome's persona, as far as Jokanaan is concerned, is not even her own – she is merely a reflection of Herodias. Jokanaan denies Salome the right to even have a persona that is identifiably hers, something at least Herod and his court grant her. His vision of her is one based on preconception; in other words, when he encounters Salome, his image of Herodias replaces any other perception he might have of her. As Austin E. Quigley notes, Jokanaan's 'unwillingness to look at a woman as beautiful as Salomé can suggest di-

65 Elliott L. Gilbert, '"Tumult of Images": Wilde, Beardsley, and *Salome*.' *Victorian Studies* 26, no. 2 (1983), 145.

66 Wilde, *Salome*, 72.

minished ability somewhere, weakness as well as strength.'[67] Jokanaan, trapped in his dark cistern, is correspondingly blinded by his idealism. By refusing to look beyond Salome's persona, he shows himself to be complicit in the patriarchal structure of the court that has defined Salome by her image.

Salome's request for Jokanaan's head is predicated upon two things: her resentment of Herod's incestuous desire for her and a more generalized resentment of the fact that she is constantly objectified, even and especially by Jokanaan. Herod, in order to cajole Salome into performing this erotic dance for him, actually gives Salome the freedom to exert her will in whatever fashion she desires. Herod's offer is in a sense a sign of defeat for Salome; unable to exert her will onto Jokanaan, Herod's offer makes it clear that the only power Salome can have access to is through her position as an object of desire. Thus her request for Jokanaan's head is a double attack against Jokanaan for refusing to see her as an individual and not just as a type of royal harlot, and against Herod for perpetuating her objectification in order to satisfy his own sexual desire for her. To Salome, both refusals to take into account her subjectivity have contributed to her request. As she says in her macabre address to the beheaded Jokanaan, 'Well, thou hast seen thy God, Jokanaan, but me, me, thou didst never see. If thou hadst seen me thou wouldst have loved me.'[68]

Salome's death, noted tersely in the play as a stage direction, ultimately points to the ambivalence Wilde shows her in the play. Wilde at once portrays Salome as uncontrollable desire while giving her a motivation for this desire. In light of this ambivalence, Salome's death appears to be less a punishment for her actions than the inevitable consequence of them. Salome dies because, like

67 Austin E. Quigley, 'Realism and Symbolism in Oscar Wilde's *Salomé*.' *Modern Drama* 37, no.1 (1994), 107.

68 Wilde, *Salome*, 91.

Dorian, a persona left unchecked cannot be sustained. And as Dorian's final hypocritical gesture towards Hetty seals his corrupt behaviour, Salome's final monologue brings the expression of her desire to completion. Yet like Dorian, Salome realizes that unbounded desire literally means that it will never be satisfied. She concedes, 'Neither the floods nor the great waters can quench my passion.'[69] Salome's desire, breaking free from the limits her persona imposed upon it, ends up consuming her as well.

69 Ibid.

Chapter Five
The Dialectic of Persona and Stereotype in the Society Comedies

In 1895, critic Clement Scott, although no admirer of Wilde, grudgingly admitted that 'Oscar Wilde is the fashion. His catch and whimsicality of dialogue tickle the public. Just now the whole of society is engaged in inventing Oscar Wildeisms.'[1] Or as Wilde's good friend Ada Leverson put it,

> It is really difficult to convey now in words the strong popularity, the craze there was at this moment for the subject of my essay; 'To meet Mr. Oscar Wilde' was put on the most exclusive of invitation cards. And every omnibus-conductor knew his latest jokes.[2]

From early 1892 until his May 1895 trials, Wilde enjoyed tremendous success as a playwright of the drawing-room comedy, a genre which took the conventions of the popular French melodramas and well-made plays of the day and recast them in a humorous vein.[3] Wilde's four drawing-room, or 'society,' comedies – *Lady Windermere's Fan* (1892), *A Woman of No Importance* (1893), *An Ideal Husband* (1895), and *The Importance of Being Earnest* (1895) – solidified Wilde's celebrity persona as the model of the sophisticate. Ironically, though, each of the comedies is about the tension surrounding an

---

1 *Illustrated London News*, 12 January 1895.

2 Ada Leverson, 'The Last First Night.' *New Criterion*, January 1926.

3 The 'well-made play' (*pièce bien-faite*) was a variation of the melodrama; Eugène Scribe was its best-known practitioner. It made extensive use of the coincidence as a plot device; frequently, conflicts were heightened and resolved through plot devices introduced specifically for this purpose.

individual's performance of the self, between working towards a self-cultivated persona and passively living as a stereotype.

Wilde's success as a playwright was inseparable from his persona, which had evolved from the sunflower-carrying aesthete to a more urbane, dandified wit. Interestingly, the perception of Wilde the sophisticated playwright was as inaccurate as the perception of his works as frothy comedies. Behind the catchy epigrams of at least the first three of his society comedies was, as Kerry Powell has pointed out, an intent to combine Ibsenite drama with the conventional well-made play. Wilde saw *Hedda Gabler* at least twice in 1891; Elizabeth Robins' performance of Hedda was, to him, 'a real masterpiece of art.'[4] William Archer's translations of Ibsen and the domestic plays they inspired offered *fin-de-siècle* English theatre an alternative to translations of French melodramas and well-made plays. Ibsen's dramas introduced London theatregoers to the 'problem play,' a drama in which the central conflict concerns an inequity or hypocrisy in society. Wilde's incorporation of the problem play into his comedies used the comedic structure as a mask – to soften the often-polarizing impact of Ibsenite drama, to conceal the more subversive elements in his plays, and to emphasize the artistic merit of these works. The structure of his society comedies, then, mimics the structure of everyday performance.

Wilde in these plays turns the concept of persona into a different sort of problem – not the symbol of a disintegrated personality in *Dorian Gray* and *Salome*, but a more social problem concerning questions of conformity, social hegemony, and the performance of everyday life. The society comedies, already more conventional than either his novel or his symbolist play, engage these questions on a serious and mimetic level even as they were best known in their time for their sparkling wit. And as a result, they interrogate their own structure by bringing up questions about the

4 Wilde, *Complete Letters*, 477.

ways in which plot and character conventions of late-Victorian popular plays have become a crude and misleading shorthand for reading culture and its practitioners.

In his comedies, Wilde reveals by concealing, using melodramatic stock characters, such as the fallen woman, the dandified rake, the moralizing *jeune fille*, and the earnest ingénue to critique the idea of a 'stock character,' and repeating them in each subsequent play. Wilde employs a level of characterization which addresses both the external problem of using stereotypical images to identify individuals and the internal struggle between these stereotypes and the desire to perform the self in an idiosyncratic way. In his comedies, he distinguishes between the static, prefixed image of a stereotype and the individual's dynamic, artistic construction of his or her identity. The idea of an individual being trapped within his or her persona, previously explored by Wilde in *Salome*, is still a concern in *Lady Windermere's Fan*, which Wilde was writing concurrently with *Salome*. In his later plays, however, the individual's persona is engaged in a tense struggle with social stereotypes, a struggle which Wilde never comfortably resolves, to the point where he keeps changing the possible resolutions in each play.

Wilde addresses two separate yet related concerns: the social criticism integral to each play and the connection constantly being made between his plays and his public persona. One common complaint among the reviewers, for instance, was that Wilde's characters all sounded the same, and they all sounded like Wilde. He never denied this charge, but managed to connect these two concerns in his comedies by making the performance of a persona the focal point in each of his plays as well as the core of the plays' social criticism. To further his point, the characters in each play can be seen as 'talking' to one another intertextually. Character dilemmas are repeated in different plays, comments and epigrams in one play are either repeated or responded to in a subsequent one. It is as if, in extending the conceit of the world being a stage, or the stage being a world in this case, each play is an aspect of the vexed relationship between a persona and a stereotype and reiterates the central criticisms Wilde makes about the relationship between the performing individual and a repressive society.

Wilde's first comedy, *Lady Windermere's Fan*, opened on 20 February 1892 at the St. James's Theatre. The play revolves around three familiar 'types' of characters: the dandies, best represented by Lord Darlington and Cecil Graham and, in feminized form, Mrs. Erlynne; the Puritans, for whom Lady Windermere is their spokeswoman; and the social set, represented primarily by the Duchess of Berwick. These characters are not only recognizable types to the audience, iterations of similar characters in other plays of the time, but recognize each other as embodiments of principles rather than as individual figures. The society Wilde portrays in *Lady Windermere's Fan* operates almost exclusively on prefixed images. Indeed, the criticism levelled against Wilde that his characters are two-dimensional does not reveal a deficiency in his abilities as a dramatist but actually points to an important aspect of a play about a fallen woman who is revealed to be the mother of a virtuous but judgmental one. Mrs. Erlynne, according to Dumby, looks 'like an *édition de luxe* of a wicked French novel, meant especially for the English market'[5] and Mrs. Erlynne does her best to conform to this image, seeing it as a commodity which she can market to a jaded social set. Lord Windermere tells his wife that Mrs. Erlynne wants to come to her party because, as he explains, 'she knows that you are a good woman – and that if she comes here once she will have a chance of a happier, a surer life than she has had.'[6] Lady Windermere's initial rejection of Mrs. Erlynne has as much to do with her compulsion to preserve her own persona as a 'good' woman as with a conventionally priggish attitude towards a fallen woman.

5 Oscar Wilde, *Lady Windermere's Fan*, in *The Importance of Being Earnest and Other Plays*, ed. Peter Raby, 1–59 (Oxford: Oxford University Press, 2008), 26.

6 Ibid., 18.

As Norbert Kohl aptly observes, Wilde's comedies (*Lady Windermere's Fan* in particular) are about dandyish figures.[7] These dandies comment cynically on the social world in which they circulate without fully engaging in it. Rather than cultivating performances which they can use to interact fully with others, the dandies in *Lady Windermere's Fan* separate themselves from the other characters. Darlington's response to Lady Windermere's charge that he had been paying her 'elaborate compliments the whole evening,' for instance, is, 'Ah, nowadays we are all of us so hard up, that the only pleasant things to pay *are* compliments. They're the only things we *can* pay.'[8] It is both a flirtatious and evasive response. Darlington is so absorbed in the performance of his dandy persona that even his sincere attentions get mistaken by Lady Windermere as part of his pose. It is notable, then, that the minute Lord Darlington immerses himself in the world by declaring his love for Lady Windermere, he ceases to make dandyish quips and instead retires into the less interesting role of the unrequited lover.

Critics, both modern and contemporary to Wilde, attribute the dandies' dialogue to Wilde inserting his own authorial voice into the play. An unsigned review in the April 1892 issue of the *Westminster Review* proclaims, 'There is no particular point about [Wilde's] characters, but they serve as mouth to enunciate the author's exquisitely funny remarks on society; and this is all that was expected of them.'[9] This is, however, an interpretation which overlooks Wilde's strategy

7 Norbert Kohl, *Oscar Wilde: The Works of a Conformist Rebel*, trans. David Henry Wilson (Cambridge: Cambridge University Press, 1989), 206.

8 Wilde, *Lady Windermere's Fan*, 8. In 1890, England suffered a minor recession due to the failure of the Bank of England's investments in Argentina, a financial crisis which not only explains Darlington's remarks but anticipates the plot of *An Ideal Husband.*

9 *Westminster Review*, April 1892. A.B. Walkley offers a concurring assessment of the play when he states, 'All the men talk like Mr. Oscar Wilde' (*Speaker*, 27 February 1892).

concerning the dandies and their performances. Darlington's forgoing of epigrams the moment he experiences a genuine emotion is Wilde's criticism of the dandy persona. Like Sibyl Vane's sudden inability to act once she falls in love, epigrams are useless to a Darlington pining for Lady Windermere's affection because they cannot signify anything but themselves. By extension, the true dandy is the living embodiment of an epigram – he can only exist outside of his own humanity. Once he experiences human emotion, he ceases to be a dandy.

Whereas Wilde's male dandies perform as a means of disengaging from society, Mrs. Erlynne performs to re-engage with the upper classes. Unlike Darlington or Cecil, Mrs. Erlynne is not strictly a dandy (although she does share both the dandy's fondness for epigrams and his suspicion of emotional bonds), since she uses her carefully-constructed persona for social-climbing purposes, displaying an ambition that a true dandy would find distasteful. Unlike the male dandies, too, Mrs. Erlynne's witticisms are directly relevant to her own situation. For instance, her comment to Lord Windermere, 'Even business should have a picturesque background. Should it not, Windermere? With a proper background women can do anything,' directly points to her own predicament even as it glories in the double entendre. [10] Mrs. Erlynne is always aware of her performance; Wilde makes it clear that she has no choice, since the performance of an adventuress persona is, more so than her attempts to blackmail Lord Windermere, her only means of re-entry into upper-class society. As she explains to her daughter,

> You don't know what it is to fall into the pit, to be despised, mocked, abandoned, sneered at – to be an outcast! to find the door shut against one, to have to creep in by hideous byways, afraid every moment lest the mask should be stripped from one's face, and all the while to hear the laughter, the

---

10 Wilde, *Lady Windermere's Fan*, 32.

> horrible laughter of the world, a thing more tragic than all the tears the world has ever shed.[11]

Mrs. Erlynne's performance as the adventuress not only develops from material circumstances but is necessary to pass in a society that, at the same time it censures a woman who artlessly and transparently reveals that she has a questionable background, is more tolerant towards a woman who merely gives the *impression* of a fallen state.

Reputedly modeled on Lillie Langtry (much to Langtry's chagrin), Mrs. Erlynne is the fallen woman and mother who manages to redeem herself by embracing neither motherhood nor death at the end of the play. As both Sos Eltis and Kerry Powell have pointed out, one of the most enduring conventions of the French melodrama was the sacrifice of the wayward mother in order to save her child. She would either consign herself to a life of good works in obscurity to atone for her previous sins or die from a mysterious illness so that her reputation will not harm her child.[12] But Mrs. Erlynne pointedly tells her son-in-law:

> I suppose, Windermere, you would like me to retire to a convent, or become a hospital nurse, or something of that kind, as people do in silly modern novels. That is stupid of you, Arthur; in real life we don't do such things – not as long as we have any good looks left, at any rate.[13]

With Mrs. Erlynne, Wilde manages to subvert two major melodramatic conventions: he refuses to sacrifice the wayward mother and, as Morse Peckham notes, he uses the final act to subvert the

---

11 Ibid., 39.

12 Sos Eltis, *Revising Wilde: Society and Subversion in the Plays of Oscar Wilde* (Oxford: Clarendon Press, 1996); Kerry Powell, *Oscar Wilde and the Theatre of the 1890s* (Cambridge: Cambridge University Press, 1990).

13 Wilde, *Lady Windermere's Fan*, 54.

reconciliation between the abandoned daughter and her mother.[14]

In *Lady Windermere's Fan*, Lady Windermere never learns of Mrs. Erlynne's true identity and never relinquishes the ideal she has of a saintly dead mother. She learns to accept Mrs. Erlynne because of her own close encounter with adultery. Mrs. Erlynne supposedly shows Lady Windermere that any woman is susceptible to sexual temptation and supposedly also redeems herself by preventing her daughter from making the same mistakes she has made. But, as Ian Gregor points out, Mrs. Erlynne's maternal gesture is bound up in her own ambitions. By protecting her daughter, she robs Lord Windermere of the motive to reveal her true identity ('outing' her, in a covert nod to the politics of the closet) and also succeeds in currying Lady Windermere's favour.[15] At the same time, however, the desire to protect Lady Windermere also provides Mrs. Erlynne with a momentary disruption to her performance as the adventuress. As she says to Lord Windermere, 'Oh, don't imagine I am going to have a pathetic scene with her, weep on her neck and tell her who I am, and all that kind of thing. I have no ambition to play the part of the mother.'[16] 'Playing the part of the mother,' as Mrs. Erlynne sees it, means substituting one role for another rather than stripping away the artifice to reveal the real mother underneath. And it is a role, unlike that of the adventuress, which causes her anguish. 'Only once in my life have I known a mother's feelings,' she says. 'That was last night. They were terrible – they made me suffer – they made me suffer too much.'[17] Motherhood for Mrs. Erlynne ends her full participation in the world. It turns her into a self-abnegating creature who exists solely for her offspring. Moreover, the persona of

14 Morse Peckham, 'What Did Lady Windermere Learn?' *College English* 18 (1956): 12.

15 Ian Gregor, 'Comedy and Oscar Wilde (1966),' in *Wilde: Comedies*, ed. William Tydeman, 111–126 (London: Macmillan, 1982), 115.

16 Wilde, *Lady Windermere's Fan*, 53–54.

17 Ibid.

the mother is all-consuming. Her role in society is to nurture her children; beyond that, she exists on its fringes, without agency and without sexuality. In the world of drama as well as the actual social world to which it refers, as Mrs. Erlynne points out, motherhood is an exit from the central action.

Wilde positions Mrs. Erlynne's persona against Lady Windermere's persona and emphasizes the hidden similarities between the two women's public images. Like Mrs. Erlynne, Lady Windermere creates her persona in order to cope with the pressures of living in upper-class society and, like her mother, Lady Windermere's persona is fragile and requires constant vigilance to maintain it. The difference between the two women, however, which Wilde uses to point out both the virtues and flaws of Lady Windermere's innocence, is Lady Windermere's professed ignorance about the constructed nature of her persona.

Throughout the play, Lady Windermere uses her 'Puritan' ideals in order to shelter herself from the realities of the world in which she lives. Her 'Puritanism' is a way to be as cynical as the dandies she distrusts while at the same time portraying her cynicism as a set of higher ideals. For instance, her comment 'London is full of women who trust their husbands. One can always recognise them. They look so thoroughly unhappy'[18] is an epigram worthy of Lord Darlington or Cecil Graham, yet Lady Windermere is seen as virtuous and innocent rather than jaded. Lady Windermere is often cynical because not only does she realize that her ideals are impossible to achieve, but she, like a cynic, is quick to assume the worst. The slightest gossip from the Duchess of Berwick immediately convinces her that Lord Windermere and Mrs. Erlynne are having an affair. Lady Windermere's ideals have no constancy; they can be dashed the moment she suspects any inconsistencies. This is the

18 Ibid., 24.

main reason behind both her initial hostility towards Mrs. Erlynne and her later acceptance of her.

Mrs. Erlynne represents to Lady Windermere her own capacity for transgression (she runs to Lord Darlington the minute she suspects her husband of philandering) and her own capacity for artifice. At the end of the play, by accepting Mrs. Erlynne, Lady Windermere offers herself forgiveness as much as her mother. If Mrs. Erlynne, the 'bad' woman, can perform a noble gesture, then Lady Windermere herself can accept the transgressive aspects of her own personality. But in order to preserve her persona as the 'good,' innocent woman, her husband and mother conspire to keep her ignorant of Mrs. Erlynne's actual identity and Lady Windermere facilitates her own ignorance by asking no questions about who Mrs. Erlynne is despite the many clues she is given. For all of Mrs. Erlynne's posturing and comments about self-cultivation, Lady Windermere can be seen to have the more artificial persona. Unlike Mrs. Erlynne, who can maintain her 'bad woman' pose with relative ease and reject the elements of her nature, such as her sudden maternal feelings, which threaten to undermine her persona, Lady Windermere constantly has to protect her 'good woman' persona from her society's influence. It is Wilde reiterating his diatribe against the natural in 'The Decay of Lying,' asserting that being natural might be the most successful pose of all, but is ultimately the least stable.

It is therefore fitting that the one character who seems to be most aware of Lady Windermere's frailties is Lord Darlington, since both characters try to hide their sensitivities from their public performances and both find themselves ultimately too cowardly to commit to the ideals, whether Puritan or dandyish, they appear to follow. Lord Darlington's impassioned speech to Lady Windermere lays bare both characters' fears:

> I won't tell you that the world matters nothing, or the world's voice, or the voice of society. They matter a great deal. They matter far too much. But

> there are moments when one has to choose between living one's own life, fully, entirely, completely – or dragging out some false, shallow, degrading existence that the world in its hypocrisy demands.[19]

With this speech, Wilde makes plain that everyone in this play is living in the closet and that your persona is the clothes you put on while in there. Darlington's romantic confession is telling only because, once denied, he retreats back, albeit into his dandy's shell, albeit with considerably less wit and vigour. Mrs. Erlynne is aware throughout the play about the dangers of revealing one's inner emotions or past identity. No one in this play seems free to cultivate their own persona according to Wilde's ideals, especially Lady Windermere who responds to Darlington's words by saying, 'I am afraid of being myself.'[20] At best, they have the choice of adopting different stereotypical roles, which leads to the central conflicts of the play: Will Mrs. Erlynne be the adventuress or the repentant mother? Will Lady Windermere be the innocent or the jaded woman? Will Lord Darlington be the dandy or the romantic lover? The play, despite its moral ending of acceptance and reconciliation, ends up being an alienating universe, where people can only survive not by pretending to be someone who they are not, but by convincing themselves that a stereotype is an acceptable substitute for agency. *Salome*, in other words, continues in *Lady Windermere's Fan*, but she has moved to the drawing rooms of upper-class London.

Wilde's second comedy, *A Woman of No Importance* – about an unrepentant rake, the young man whom he mentors and who, unbeknownst to him, is his illegitimate son, and the former lover who was left pregnant and jilted and was forced to pretend to be a widow and raise her son in obscurity – opened in April 1893 at the Haymarket Theatre under the production of actor-manager Herbert Beerbohm Tree, who also played the role of the rakish Lord

19 Ibid., 28–29.

20 Ibid, 29.

Illingworth. Beerbohm Tree had already established his professional reputation by playing witty aristocrats, such as the role of a duke in Henry Arthur Jones's *The Dancing Girl* that he performed just prior to staging Wilde's play, and he meant for the role of Lord Illingworth to solidify his public persona.

Lord Illingworth is a rewriting of Lord Henry Wotton. Wilde gives several of Lord Henry's lines verbatim to Lord Illingworth, such as his comment about how it is 'perfectly monstrous the way people go about, nowadays, saying things against one behind one's back that are absolutely and entirely true'[21] and his description of women as 'Sphinxes without secrets.'[22] In addition, Lord Illingworth's relationship with his son Gerald Arbuthnot has overtones similar to Lord Henry's influence over Dorian Gray. Lord Illingworth fascinates Gerald as Lord Henry fascinates Dorian; Lord Illingworth, Gerald says, 'knows more about life than any one I have ever met.'[23] The impetus to revisit Lord Henry and all of his dangerous philosophies may have been actuated by the Lord Chamberlain's decision to ban performances of *Salome* in England only weeks before Wilde began writing *A Woman of No Importance*. The play's title ironically echoes Salome's predicament in Herod's court. Moreover, *A Woman of No Importance* reintroduces the theme of the rigid, immutable persona in comedic (and non-Biblical) form. The social world of *A Woman of No Importance* is as cruel and unforgiving as the world of both *The Picture of Dorian Gray* and *Salome*, and persona is used in all of these works as a means of survival in nearly a social Darwinist sense. As Lord Illingworth demonstrates, one can

---

21 Oscar Wilde, *A Woman of No Importance*, in *The Importance of Being Earnest and Other Plays*, ed. Peter Raby, 93–157 (Oxford: Oxford University Press, 2008), 104; Wilde, *The Picture of Dorian Gray*, 138.

22 Wilde, *A Woman of No Importance*, 110; Wilde, *The Picture of Dorian Gray*, 152.

23 Wilde, *A Woman of No Importance*, 125.

use one's persona as a way of dominating society's weaker, or more innocent, members.

The main conflict of *A Woman of No Importance* is not introduced until Mrs. Arbuthnot, Gerald's mother and Lord Illingworth's former lover, makes her first appearance well into the second act. This delay in the entrance of a major character, unique among his plays, allows Wilde to foreground the social context which determines both the actions and the motivations of his principal characters. In an 1895 interview with Gilbert Burgess for *The Sketch*, Wilde claimed, 'I wrote the first act of *A Woman of No Importance* in answer to the critics who said that *Lady Windermere's Fan* lacked action. In the act in question there was absolutely no action at all. It was a perfect act.'[24] The effect of Wilde's first act is both theatrically aesthetic and morally disturbing. The first act might be an artistic tableau with dialogue, but the gossip which replaces the action reveals the heartlessness and cruelty of Hustanton Chase. The society in this play is the same society as the one portrayed in *Lady Windermere's Fan*, but the members here are even more attuned to superficialities, even more self-obsessed and even more oblivious to the people surrounding them. Lady Caroline makes a special point of this obliviousness when she continually mispronounces Kelvil's (the philanthropic Member of Parliament's) name. Social and moral issues are introduced in the first act of *A Woman of No Importance* as the butts of Lady Caroline's or Lord Illingworth's jokes, but the effect of this mockery is that, in an age of increased social awareness, the social set in the play is seen as outdated.

The problem of the society in *A Woman of No Importance* is similar to the one that Wilde emphasizes in *Lady Windermere's Fan*, and it is one which emerges out of the tension between the stagnant stereotype and the dynamic performance. However, in *A Woman of No Importance*, the tension has fossilized into a state where the

24 Gilbert Burgess, 'A Talk with Mr. Oscar Wilde,' *The Sketch*, 9 January 1895.

stereotype has successfully overshadowed the performance. Unlike the characters in *Lady Windermere's Fan*, such as Mrs. Erlynne who reveals a momentary maternal streak under her adventuress' mask, or Lady Windermere who comes to understand that a virtuous woman is a compassionate one, the characters in *A Woman of No Importance* are already hardened in their moulds. There is neither nuance nor the possibility for change for Lord Illingworth, for example. He does not have any dialectical relationship to his own persona and therefore is bound by his role as a rake. Mrs. Arbuthnot, as well, has taken the persona she had to adopt when Gerald was born, that of the sacrificing widow and mother, and behaves according to that role.

As Peter Raby suggests, the introduction of social and political issues into the play form 'a parallel to the analysis of relationships between men and women.'[25] A large part of the tension in the play comes from the power struggle between the sexes, which assumes similar dimensions to the class struggle. Like the relationship between the upper and lower classes, the banter between Lord Illingworth and Mrs. Allonby demonstrate that, although the two sexes coexist in the same space, they fundamentally operate as two solitudes:

> LORD ILLINGWORTH. So much marriage is certainly not becoming. Twenty years of romance make a woman look like a ruin; but twenty years of marriage make her something like a public building.
>
> MRS. ALLONBY. Twenty years of romance! Is there such a thing?
>
> LORD ILLINGWORTH. Not in our day. Women have become too brilliant. Nothing spoils a romance so much as a sense of humour in the woman.
>
> MRS. ALLONBY. Or the want of it in the man.

25 Peter Raby, 'Wilde's Comedies of Society' in *The Cambridge Companion to Oscar Wilde*, ed. Peter Raby, 143–160 (Cambridge: Cambridge University Press, 1997), 154.

LORD ILLINGWORTH. You are quite right. In a Temple every one should be serious, except the thing that is worshipped.

MRS. ALLONBY. And that should be man?

LORD ILLINGWORTH. Women kneel so gracefully; men don't.[26]

Tellingly, both parties use their wit to deny the other sex access to knowledge about themselves. Lord Illingworth says outrageously misogynist things to Mrs. Allonby and she encourages him, because as long as he relies on a stereotypical view of women, she is protected from him obtaining any real knowledge of her. Lord Illingworth and Mrs. Allonby manipulate their types, a rake and a sophisticate, like two battle strategists mobilizing their troops. They use these stereotypes rather than their personalities in order to avoid direct engagement with each other. In this way, they are like the dandies of *Lady Windermere's Fan*, but they demonstrate in a more urgent and less figurative sense a keener awareness that their images are weapons.

But characters such as Lord Illingworth and Mrs. Allonby were not the ones that irked the first reviewers of *A Woman of No Importance*. For many reviewers, Mrs. Arbuthnot and Hester Worsley, the American *jeune fille* character, were the most unbelievable and unlikeable characters in the play. William Archer in his 1893 review dismissed Mrs. Arbuthnot's anger as hyperbolic, stating that she

> is simply a woman who has been through a very painful experience, who has suffered a crushing disappointment in the unworthiness of the man she loves, but for whom life, after all, has turned out not so very intolerably.[27]

The idea that Mrs. Arbuthnot was not punished in the manner of the fallen women of melodrama meant to critics such as Archer that

---

26 Wilde, *A Woman of No Importance*, 109.

27 *World*, 26 April 1893.

she ought to be grateful for her relatively fortunate situation. Mrs. Arbuthnot's resentment, however, is based on the sacrifice of her persona and independence in the service of her son, a sacrifice obviously not made by Lord Illingworth. Like Mrs. Erlynne, Mrs. Arbuthnot resents the hold motherhood has on her life and on her identity. In order to maintain a respectable reputation for her son, Mrs. Arbuthnot has had to sacrifice her future in order to maintain the persona of a grieving and chaste widow. Moreover, she makes it clear in the play that this persona of the widow was not even offered to her as a choice. The rigidity of society and its insistence on seeing an unwed mother as a certain type of woman made it impossible for her to adopt any other course than to step away from the world so that her son may live in it without being socially ostracized.

If Mrs. Arbuthnot aroused scepticism in the reviewers, Hester incited them to bouts of ire. An anonymous 'open letter' to Wilde, appearing in the *Theatre* in June 1893, carped that

> Hester Worsley is the dismallest of figures. She is not even a woman, let alone a typical woman, and certainly is not typical of any phase of womanhood known in America. She is a literal translation from the French, a bloodless, mechanical *jeune personne* of Scribe and Sardou.[28]

Hester's unforgiveable flaw, according to this reviewer, is that she is a flat representation of a stock character in French melodrama, the 'young person' who is the unflinching moral voice of the play. In Hester, though, Wilde combines the judgmental qualities of the *jeune personne* or *fille* with the romantic role of the *ingénue*. Hester is depicted as a prophet, like Jokanaan or Wilde himself in 'The Soul of Man under Socialism,' looking down (literally, at one point) on the Hustanton Chase set and proclaiming in Biblical intonations their sins:

28 *Theatre*, 1 June 1893.

> You love the beauty that you can see and touch and handle, the beauty that you can destroy, and do destroy, but of the unseen beauty of life, of the unseen beauty of a higher life, you know nothing. You have lost life's secret. Oh, your English society seems to me shallow, selfish, foolish. It has blinded its eyes, and stopped its ears. It lies like a leper in purple. It sits like a dead thing smeared with gold. It is all wrong, all wrong.[29]

This speech to Lady Hustanton is especially reminiscent of Jokanaan's rants in the cistern. But Hester, like Jokanaan and like the people whom she denounces, is also guilty of stereotyping. She states:

> If a man and woman have sinned, let them both go forth into the desert to love and loathe each other there. Let them both be branded. Set a mark, if you wish, on each, but don't punish the one and let the other go free. Don't have one law for men and another for women.[30]

While on the surface this speech appears to be somewhat progressive, in that Hester advocates the destruction of a sexual double standard, Wilde implies that she also advocates a univocal, unyielding system of justice, one which punishes the individual's deeds without taking into account the individual's intentions. Hester may disrupt the heartlessness of the upper class in the play, but her solutions are not any more tenable, something which is pointed out by Lady Caroline's snide obliviousness to Hester's impassioned speech. And Hester's rigidity is not sustained within the play's conventional comedic ending; she contradicts herself by embracing the fallen woman and her illegitimate son.

In *A Woman of No Importance*, Wilde offers his audience an alternate universe to the one in *Lady Windermere's Fan*, a world where there is no possibility for a dialectical relationship between the self and its persona. Unlike Mrs. Erlynne, for example, who is aware of her struggle with the clashing personae of adventuress and mother,

29 Wilde, *A Woman of No Importance*, 119.

30 Ibid., 120.

Mrs. Arbuthnot is completely locked into her persona as a sacrificing mother. Indeed, Mrs. Arbuthnot secures for herself a happy ending by not developing as a character and by not allowing her son to develop either. Similarly, both Hester and Lord Illingworth remain the same at the end of the play, pointing to the pessimism at the heart of the comedy. Like the world of *Salome*, the world of *A Woman of No Importance* is unable to break away from its dependence on stereotypical images. The only recourse for characters such as Lord Illingworth and Mrs. Arbuthnot is to adhere so faithfully to their personae that they end up perverting them; the only recourse for younger characters such as Gerald and Hester is to leave. Hustanton Chase does not end in chaos as does Herod's court; instead, genteel-like, it ends up in a state of attrition. But both societies are dying and the new states will be ones that belong, Wilde implies somewhat idealistically, to those who champion the development of the individual – the Christians in *Salome*'s world who will combat the decadence of Herod's court through their reverence of Wilde's concept of Christ as the epitome of the individual and the 'modern' family of Gerald, Hester, and Mrs. Arbuthnot who will flourish in the more egalitarian America.

In *An Ideal Husband* (produced by actor-manager Lewis Waller at the Haymarket Theatre in January 1895), Wilde for the first time since his failed 1880 play *Vera* used actual political events as a source for his play. The possible selling of government secrets and the speculation on the building of an intercoastal canal have their roots in two separate occurrences. In 1875, Disraeli borrowed a large sum of money from the Rothschilds to purchase the Khedive of Egypt's shares in the Suez Canal on behalf of the British government, an action he undertook without the consent of Parliament. In 1889, after nine years of attempting to build a canal through Panama, the French-based Panama Canal Company folded, scandalizing the French government. In fact, as Wilde was writing *An Ideal Husband*, a second organization had been formed by the French government to continue work on the Panama Canal. Wilde uses these events as the basis for Sir Robert Chiltern's morally suspect past – that he sold government secrets early in his political career to the Mephistophelean Baron Arnheim, was rewarded by his patron with a mercurial rise in politics, and is now being blackmailed by Mrs. Cheveley, the Baron's old friend, to endorse a sham canal scheme in the House of Commons.

An Ideal Husband is technically a society comedy, but the world of social gatherings is portrayed as a mirror image of political life, and as Wilde depicts them, both require individuals to perform specific personae in order to succeed. As Peter Raby notes, 'the idea of "real" life as theatre is especially powerful' in *An Ideal Husband*.[31] And as E.H. Mikhail claims, 'Wilde's preoccupation with masks as symbols begins positively to shout.'[32] In *An Ideal Husband* Wilde examines how one's persona can, in the case of Lord Goring, conceal one's interior life or, in the case of Sir Robert Chiltern and Mrs. Cheveley, help to construct it. One's persona is truly a mask in *An Ideal Husband*, an artificial construction bearing an arbitrary resemblance to the inner self. Lord Goring demonstrates the artificiality of his persona when he unwittingly reveals that beneath his 'heartless,' dandyish surface is a compassionate but rather conservative morality. Conversely, Sir Robert Chiltern's persona as the rare man of integrity in politics gives way to reveal his nearly amoral ambition. Like Wilde's earlier comedies, where the persona one is required to perform is at odds with the persona one may wish to perform, the tension in *An Ideal Husband* emerges out of the discrepancy between these two kinds of personae. Unlike the earlier comedies, however, this theme is made explicit in *An Ideal Husband*, beginning with the title of the play itself. The 'ideal' in question is the image one pro-

---

31 Raby, 'Wilde's Comedies of Society,' 158.

32 E.H. Mikhail, 'Self-Revelation in *An Ideal Husband*.' *Modern Drama* 11, no. 2 (1968), 181.

jects and also the ideal of long-held convictions, or the ideal that Mrs. Erlynne in *Lady Windermere's Fan* likens to an illusion. This latter definition is provided by Lady Chiltern, who cannot accept the idea of Sir Robert's persona as a false indicator of his interior life.

Lady Chiltern does not distinguish between Sir Robert's public and private lives. For her, Sir Robert's success in matrimony depends on his conduct as a politician. As Ian Gregor notes, 'Corruption in the one sphere is, for her, corruption in the other.'[33] In *An Ideal Husband*, Lady Chiltern's illusions are held to be more valuable, and ultimately truer, than reality. More so, and even more cynically than in Wilde's previous comedies, a persona is the only means by which an individual can be identified. In *An Ideal Husband*, however, one's persona is the result of one's will rather than a reaction to a socially-determined stereotype and, especially in the cases of Sir Robert, Mrs. Cheveley and Baron Arnheim, a persona is the face of Dorian Gray, concealing the rotting interior underneath. In addition, the use of a persona as the medium for interpersonal relationships is a conscious choice made by the characters, particularly Lady Chiltern, who uses her own persona as the 'good woman' to perpetuate Sir Robert's superficial persona as both an 'ideal husband' and a respected politician.

For Wilde, the political persona is no different from an artistic pose. From the first stage directions, Wilde sets the actions of the play in the world of art even as the plot unfolds as a political drama. Whereas the stage directions in his other comedies are merely functional, the directions in *An Ideal Husband* (most of which Wilde added in 1899 for the published copy of the play) include character descriptions which explicitly liken them to works of art.[34] The opening stage directions state:

---

33 Gregor, 'Comedy and Oscar Wilde,' 117.

34 Russell Jackson, 'Horrible Flesh and Blood – A Rejoinder.' *Theatre Notebook* 37, no. 1 (1983): 30–31. In her article 'Horrible Flesh and Blood' (*Theatre*

> *Mrs. Marchmont and Lady Basildon, two very pretty women, are seated together on a Louis Seize sofa. They are types of exquisite fragility. Their affectation of manner has a delicate charm. Watteau would have loved to paint them.*[35]

The stage directions later describe Mabel Chiltern as being

> *a perfect example of the English type of prettiness, the apple-blossom type. . . . To sane people she is not reminiscent of any work of art. But she is really like a Tanagra statuette, and would be rather annoyed if she were told so.*[36]

The 'sane' people Wilde cheekily comments about is not just a reference to Philistinism, given the amount of criticism Wilde levels at a society that is hostile to any persona other than the most stereotypical ones. Mabel replicates this comment (and presages Gwendolen and Cecily) when she articulates an ironic relationship to her own stereotypical look and stage persona as the ingénue.

The description of Sir Robert states:

Notebook 35, no. 1 [1981]), Kristin Morrison argues that Wilde adopted the use of lengthy stage directions after reading Shaw's plays, especially *Widowers' Houses*. Alan Andrews, in his response to Morrison's article ('Horrible Flesh and Blood,' *Theatre Notebook* 36, no.1 [1982]), points out that the lengthy stage directions could only have come from the published version of Shaw's play, since the acting copy of *Widowers' Houses* that Wilde read had very sparse stage directions and, as Jackson confirms in his later article, could only have been included in *An Ideal Husband* in a later published edition. Jackson, however, does note that, judging from the typescript of the play given to New York impresario Daniel Frohman, the stage darkening at the end of Act One and the use of candles and shades off-stage in Act Three were used in the original production of the play.

35 Oscar Wilde, *An Ideal Husband*, in *The Importance of Being Earnest and Other Plays*, ed. Peter Raby, 159–245 (Oxford: Oxford University Press, 2008), 165.

36 Ibid., 166.

> *It would be inaccurate to call him picturesque. Picturesqueness cannot survive the House of Commons. But Vandyck would have liked to have painted his head.*[37]

Donald Ericksen notes that each of the artists Wilde uses to describe his characters 'throughout or at some stage of his career represents a commitment to artificiality, sensuosity, and escapism.'[38] The notion of art as escapism is used ironically or perhaps even wistfully by Wilde, since even as he places characters in an 'escapist' world of art, his play is concerned with the impossibility of ever escaping oneself. Sir Robert comes to his career as a politician through aesthetics, and particularly through an aesthetic sensibility that sees political power as the ultimate art form. His relationship with Baron Arnheim, the mysterious foreign financier, is reminiscent of Gerald Arbuthnot's initial attitude towards Lord Illingworth in *A Woman of No Importance* and Dorian Gray's early relationship with Lord Henry Wotton.

Sir Robert describes the Baron as 'a man of a most subtle and refined intellect. A man of culture, charm, and distinction. One of the most intellectual men I ever met.'[39] Baron Arnheim's political acumen, wealth, and ruthlessness are indistinguishable from his aestheticism. Combined, these traits form a persona which induces Sir Robert to risk his integrity (his political 'soul') in order to emulate the Baron. The generalized corruption of Dorian Gray becomes a more specifically political corruption in *An Ideal Husband.* Sir Robert's description of the Baron's 'seduction' takes place in a setting echoing Dorian Gray's apartments and involves language reminiscent of Lord Henry:

> I remember so well how, with a strange smile on his pale, curved lips, he led me through his wonderful picture gallery, showed me his tapestries, his

---

37 Ibid., 168.

38 Donald H. Ericksen, *Oscar Wilde* (Boston: Twayne, 1977), 144.

39 Wilde, *An Ideal Husband*, 192.

enamels, his jewels, his carved ivories, made me wonder at the strange loveliness of the luxury in which he lived; and then told me that luxury was nothing but a background, a painted scene in a play, and that power, power over other men, power over the world, was the one thing worth having, the one supreme pleasure worth knowing, the one joy one never tired of, and that in our century only the rich possessed it.[40]

Sir Robert, though he responds to the Baron's persona, ultimately cannot emulate him because a persona influenced by Baron Arnheim clashes with Lady Chiltern's political and domestic ideal of her husband. As she reminds her husband, the public and the private 'should both represent man at his highest. I see no difference between them.'[41] Ironically, it is Lady Chiltern's idealistic conception of Sir Robert and his efforts to cultivate a persona based on these ideals which threaten to destroy his career and marriage. Lady Chiltern is as guilty as the socialites in *Lady Windermere's Fan* and *A Woman of No Importance* in that she typecasts Sir Robert as the 'ideal husband,' a role which, as Mrs. Allonby in *A Woman of No Importance* reminds us, does not exist except as a figment of women's imagination.

In the play's ambivalent 'happy ending,' Mrs. Cheveley is conveniently disposed of before she can fulfill her threats, Sir Robert's marriage, career and reputation remain intact, and Lady Chiltern comes to peace with Sir Robert's past thanks to Lord Goring's intervention on Sir Robert's behalf. In an earlier draft of the play, however, Lady Chiltern reacts to the news of Sir Robert's past by running into Lord Goring's arms (echoing Lady Windermere's near-scandal); Lord Goring uses that opportunity to lecture Lady Chiltern on human weakness and on her own capacity for forgiveness.[42] The earlier draft of the play, while more conventionally melodramatic, makes the argument that Sir Robert's failings

40 Ibid, 192–193.

41 Ibid., 186.

42 Eltis, *Revising Wilde*, 144.

are symptoms of his humanity, failings which Lady Chiltern shares and which she therefore is in no position to judge. The final version of the play, however, portrays Lady Chiltern as morally stainless who forgives her husband due to Lord Goring's clever entreaty that, by doing so, she can become a feminine ideal, a paragon of unconditional love. 'What sort of existence will he have,' Lord Goring admonishes her,

> if you rob him of the fruits of his ambition, if you take him from the splendour of a great political career, if you close the doors of public life against him, if you condemn him to sterile failure, he who was made for triumph and success? Women are not meant to judge us, but to forgive us when we need forgiveness. Pardon, not punishment is their mission. . . . A man's life is of more value than a woman's. It has larger issues, wider scope, greater ambitions. A woman's life revolves in curves of emotion. It is upon the lines of intellect that a man's life progresses. . . . A woman who can keep a man's love, and love him in return, has done all the world wants of women, or should want of them.[43]

What Lord Goring gives Lady Chiltern in this speech is a static, idealized image of womanhood, one which Lady Chiltern adopts as her persona and is therefore able to forgive Sir Robert his transgressions. Wilde realizes that in order to forgive Sir Robert, Lady Chiltern must be put into a position where she willingly adopts a persona which is not only blatantly improbable but an iteration of a Victorian man's idealized fantasy of women. Reactionary though it may be, Lady Chiltern, in order to perpetuate both her marriage and her lifestyle, must become an ideal herself; in doing so, the Chilterns manage to dispense with the morality that necessitated the 'horrible painted masks' being worn throughout the play. As Kerry Powell points out, the result of Lady Chiltern's change of heart is a 'patched-together happy ending' which is 'at the same time subver-

43 Wilde, *An Ideal Husband*, 241–242.

sive and dramatically unconvincing.'[44] In short, Sir Robert gets away with his misdeeds and Lady Chiltern ignores the moral convictions that had structured her identity.

An Ideal Husband is the culmination of the potential catastrophe looming in both *Lady Windermere's Fan* and *A Woman of No Importance.* In the previous two comedies, the conflict arose out of a tension between persona and stereotype. This dialectic is resolved in the plays either by some degree of synthesis – Mrs. Erlynne's brief incorporation of maternal tenderness, for instance, which leads her to become a more sympathetic character than the stereotypical adventuress (and reclaimed by Dumby back into genteel society) yet not quite the suffering mother expected of another stereotype – or by a rigid, old-fashioned character, such as Lord Illingworth, being foiled by more 'modern' personae. *An Ideal Husband*, however, dispenses with the dialectic altogether in the end. The vexed relationship between persona (and the performance it entails) and stereotype is seen to be potentially disastrous for both public and private life, so persona is ceded in favour of a wholehearted embrace of the stereotype. It is Wilde's most pessimistic play where not even the romance between the two dandyish characters, Mabel and Lord Goring (both trapped, as Wilde's dandies are, in their own carefully-constructed personae), can alleviate the sense that the cultivation and performance of persona, so lovingly described and championed by Wilde, is ultimately a doomed endeavour, and that the tyranny of social norms and the stereotypes that are their main articulation will prevail over the individual and his or her persona.

However, Wilde's last and best-known comedy offers one last rebuttal to the conclusions offered by *An Ideal Husband. The Importance of Being Earnest* opened in February 1895 at the St. James's Theatre, with George Alexander playing the part of Jack Worthing.[45]

---

44 Powell, *Oscar Wilde and the Theatre of the 1890s*, 87.

45 Alexander was the one who convinced Wilde to trim the planned four-act

The comedy received an extremely warm critical reception; Hamilton Frye, the drama critic of the London *Times*, spoke for most of the reviewers when he wrote that 'Oscar Wilde may be said to have at last, and by a single stroke, put his enemies under his feet.'[46] After having written three comedies, and after having read the critics' complaints that the comedies were rehashes of various French melodramas, that the characters all sounded alike and all sounded like the playwright, Wilde wrote a comedy that flouted both the warmed-over French melodrama of the London stage and the bleak naturalism of the Ibsenite New Drama that had become the standard for 'serious' works of theatre. Indeed, *Earnest*'s comedy is rooted in metatheatre. Its discourse is a parody of other plays, both melodrama and New Drama, and its situations and characters are subversions of other dramatic works. As the characters are mocking various performative acts, Wilde is playing with formal conventions of contemporary theatre. For instance, Wilde got rid of the 'curtain' of conventional drama, the tableau scene where the characters freeze in their poses as the curtain lowers at the end of each act. He replaced the 'curtain' with 'the casual, go-as-you-please fashion of the ultra-naturalistic school,'[47] ending each act with dialogue rather than a tableau.

The confusion between the infant Jack and Miss Prism's lost manuscript, as Kerry Powell notes, is a reference to the metaphor

---

version of *Earnest* down to three acts. The four-act version often seen in collected works of Wilde is not in fact Wilde's original draft; rather, it is a reconstruction made by Vyvyan Holland based on production notes from an early German staging of the play as well as production notes from the London performances. The edition used here is the three-act version of *The Importance of Being Earnest.*

46 *Times*, 17 February 1895. George Bernard Shaw's complaint that *Earnest* is a 'heartless' play is perhaps the most memorable of the comedy's contemporary reviews, but Shaw's was a minority view.

47 *Fortnightly Review*, 1 May 1908.

Lövborg makes between his manuscript and a child in *Hedda Gabler*.[48] The parodies of the New Drama are also parodies of the naturalistic elements in Wilde's own comedies, namely the social criticism that underscores each of those plays. The theatre reviews of Wilde's time tended to undervalue the earlier comedies, focusing on their supposed derivativeness and either overlooking or deriding the social commentary. In *Earnest*, Wilde parodies the critical reception of his earlier plays as much as he parodies both the melodramatic and the naturalistic conventions of his work. The recognition scene between Jack and Miss Prism, for example, pokes fun at the conventional reunion between the outcast mother and her abandoned child, a moment he also denied the audience in *Lady Windermere's Fan* and *A Woman of No Importance*:

> JACK (*in a pathetic voice*). Miss Prism, more is restored to you than this hand-bag. I was the baby you placed in it.
>
> MISS PRISM (*amazed*). You?
>
> JACK (*embracing her*). Yes . . . mother!
>
> MISS PRISM (*recoiling in indignant astonishment*). Mr. Worthing, I am unmarried!
>
> JACK. Unmarried! I do not deny that is a serious blow. But after all, who has the right to cast a stone against one who has suffered? Cannot repentance wipe out an act of folly? Why should there be one law for men, and another for women? Mother, I forgive you.[49]

As Russell Jackson notes, the woman with a past becomes Miss Prism whose guilty behaviour is simply absent-mindedness; the

---

48 Powell, *Oscar Wilde and the Theatre of the 1890s*, 76.

49 Oscar Wilde, *The Importance of Being Earnest*, in *The Importance of Being Earnest and Other Plays*, ed. Peter Raby, 247–307 (Oxford: Oxford University Press, 2008), 305.

great secret of the play is a handbag; and the villainous or virtuous dandy becomes a dandy with no moral point at all.[50] Moreover, as both Arthur Ganz and Ian Gregor note, the dandy in *Earnest* is neither subordinate to nor even in conflict with the Philistine element of society. In the world of *Earnest*, actually, where forms of behaviour and modes of performance become the things through which one ascertains meaning, the dandy is the ideal figure.[51] Jack and Algernon are able to manipulate the rules of social behaviour by *reduction ad absurdum*, deconstructing the language of manners until, as in Shakespeare's comedies, they make the social rules conform to their own desires. Bunburying is the comedy's best example of life as theatre, in which a melodramatic situation is contrived in order for an individual to engage in some secret play and to avoid participation in play or a ritual not to his liking. With Bunbury, a performance like attending a tedious family dinner party is merely replaced with a performance more to Algernon and Jack's liking, such as running up considerable debts in the London clubs.[52]

In *The Importance of Being Earnest*, Wilde answers his critics by writing a comedy which is an exaggerated representation of the critics' perceptions of Wilde – trivial, paradoxical, witty, and ultimately frivolous. Indeed, many of the critics, in praising the comedy, saw it as a transparent representation of Wilde's personality. The reviewer for the newspaper *Truth* claimed:

> But I have no doubt in my own mind that the chief reason why the St. James's piece proves so amusing, is because it is so completely dominated by

50 Russell Jackson, '*The Importance of Being Earnest*.' In *The Cambridge Companion to Oscar Wilde*, ed. Peter Raby, 161–177 (Cambridge: Cambridge University Press, 1997), 166.

51 See Gregor, 'Comedy and Oscar Wilde,' 119, and Arthur Ganz, 'The Meaning of *The Importance of Being Earnest*.' *Modern Drama* 6, no. 1 (1963), 49.

52 The four-act version includes an arrest of Jack's brother 'Ernest' (impersonated by Algernon at this point) for non-payment of debts.

its author. That is to say, there is no attempt in it at characterisation, but all the *dramatis personae*, from the heroes down to their butlers, talk pure and undiluted Wildese.[53]

William Archer, the critic and Ibsen champion who had previously given *A Woman of No Importance* a thorough and respectful review, found *Earnest* 'delightful,' but apparently beyond the purview of criticism:

What can a poor critic do with a play which raises no principle, whether of art or morals, creates its own canons and conventions, and is nothing but an absolutely wilful expression of an irrepressibly witty personality?[54]

With *Earnest*, Wilde took the criticisms of his earlier plays – that all the characters ended up sounding just like him – and turned it into one of the themes. In fact, *Earnest* is Wilde's only play in which the critics are correct about the singularity of voice, because the play is about the triumph of persona, an aptly idealistic outcome for a play that is the least mimetic of all of Wilde's society comedies. The characters create fictitious images of themselves which miraculously become true representations at the end of the play.

In *The Importance of Being Earnest*, the struggle between the individual's performance of his persona and the society that wishes to dictate its shape which is the basis for nearly all of Wilde's writings since *The Picture of Dorian Gray* comes to an absurd and subversive resolution. Jack, for instance, can appear to be an upright citizen because of his creation of a rakish and dissolute younger brother, a brother who turns out to actually exist. Cecily's romantic fantasy about a marriage between herself and Jack's younger brother comes to pass, Algernon's Bunburying translates into becoming the real manifestation of Jack's 'Bunbury,' and, through the happy discovery

53 *Truth*, 21 February 1895.

54 *World*, 20 February 1895.

of the Army List, Gwendolen's ideal lover Ernest becomes her actual lover. The characters blithely defy the assumptions in Wilde's previous play that society will ultimately dictate your persona; in *Earnest*, individual will and desire trump social limitations.

Wilde extends the argument he made in his previous works that individuals live and function within a world of illusions and ideals. Every character in *The Importance of Being Earnest* operates within a conventional narrative or dramatic genre: Cecily constructs a romantic narrative for herself and Algernon, Gwendolen lives within a comedy of manners, Jack the orphan, like the similarly-named hero of countless fairy tales, has to overcome a series of obstacles in order to marry Gwendolen, and Algernon tricks his way into the *fin-de-siècle* narrative of the double identity. However, unlike Lady Windermere or Lady Chiltern, for example, these characters choose the narratives they inhabit. The characters in *The Importance of Being Earnest* see themselves as characters in their own plays; therefore, their performances (distinguished, as Algernon notes at the beginning of the play, by their enthusiasm rather than accuracy) construct their reality.

Each character's performance is an absurd rendition of the characters of Wilde's earlier plays. Algernon is the rake, for instance, but his appetite has been reduced from a sexual to a literal one – he cannot stop eating cucumber sandwiches or muffins. Jack's creation of the imaginary younger brother and his own eventual metamorphosis into Ernest parodies the orphan's fluid identity (such as that of Gerald Arbuthnot) in Victorian literature. Gwendolen parodies the rigid, idealistic 'good women' of Wilde's previous comedies, but her ideals are reduced to the meaningless signifier of a man's first name:

> My ideal has always been to love some one of the name of Ernest. There is something in that name that inspires absolute confidence. The moment

> Algernon first mentioned to me that he had a friend called Ernest, I knew I was destined to love you.[55]

The idealism of Lady Windermere and Lady Chiltern has been reduced to a fetish and an ironic commentary.

Cecily, like Hester Worsley, is serious and moralistic, exhibiting traits of the *jeune fille* of French melodrama. However, unlike Hester, Cecily's moral beliefs are built upon the paradoxical language of the epigram. 'I hope you have not been leading a double life, pretending to be wicked and being really good all the time,' she sternly tells Algernon. 'That would be hypocrisy.'[56] Cecily constantly substitutes the literal for the figurative: 'I am not little,' she objects to Algernon calling her his 'little cousin.' 'In fact, I believe I am more than usually tall for my age.'[57] Even more so than the other characters, Cecily's speech is essentially performative. To paraphrase J.L. Austin, she does things with words. [58] She desires to be the heroine of a romance and realizes this desire simply by articulating it; the act of speaking or writing in her diary causes the action to come into being. In the second act, Algernon falls in love and becomes engaged to Cecily after she reads him her fictive diary entries about her romance and subsequent engagement to the imaginary Ernest. And like Wilde's other *jeune fille* character, Cecily's relative 'innocence' barely conceals a bit of a hypocritical core. Hester's moralizing, for instance, directs the audience away from the fact that as she is reprimanding the upper classes, she is also enjoying their hospitality and her criticisms of Lord Illingworth and Mrs. Arbuthnot's youthful

---

55 Wilde, *The Importance of Being Earnest*, 262.

56 Ibid., 275.

57 Ibid.

58 I am using J.L. Austin's definition of 'performative speech' as a situation where 'the issuing of the utterance is the performing of the action.' J.L. Austin, 'How To Do Things With Words,' in *Literary Theory: An Anthology*, ed. Julie Rivkin and Michael Ryan, 162–176 (Oxford: Blackwell, 2004), 163.

passion are suspect given her own passion for Gerald.[59] Similarly, Cecily's role as an ingénue does not account for her cunning manipulation of Algernon. But her role is so enthusiastically performed that the performance becomes sincere and influences Algernon's performance, who finds himself playing the reformed rake and begging Cecily's forgiveness.

Of course, the most memorable character in the play is Lady Bracknell, even though, when compared to the number of lines spoken by the four young lovers, her role is relatively minor. Lady Bracknell was as much a conventional theatrical type as the other characters, one whose roots go back at least to Congreve's Lady Wishfort. Rose Leclercq, the original Lady Bracknell, was so cast because of her experience playing similar parts. Like Beerbohm Tree's performance of Lord Illingworth, Leclercq's casting ensured instant audience recognition and understanding of Lady Bracknell's character. In fact, John Stokes argues that she may have distracted the audience from her performance by unwittingly reminding it of her previous roles.[60]

As the play's representative of social hegemony, Lady Bracknell's flexibility towards social norms and the language of etiquette is at the heart of Wilde's social criticism. Lady Bracknell's very literalness renders her verbal pronouncements solely theatrical and negates any real reference point. Her famous exchange with Jack takes the form of intonations of his responses (Jack: I was found / Lady Bracknell: Found!; Jack: In a hand-bag. / Lady Bracknell: A hand-bag?),[61] leading to a delightfully absurd analogy with a question whose answer may likely and self-reflexively be the 'Reign of Terror':

59 Eltis, *Revising Wilde*, 119.

60 John Stokes, *Oscar Wilde: Myths, Miracles, and Imitations* (Cambridge: Cambridge Univ. Press, 1996), 171.

61 Wilde, *The Importance of Being Earnest*, 266.

> Mr. Worthing, I confess I feel somewhat bewildered by what you have just told me. To be born, or at any rate bred, in a hand-bag, whether it had handles or not, seems to me to display a contempt for the ordinary decencies of family life that reminds one of the worst excesses of the French Revolution. And I presume you know what that unfortunate movement led to?[62]

Lady Bracknell may or may not have been modelled after Queen Victoria; what is more apparent is that she does represent a stereotype of Victoria in her old age and thus depicts social authority in caricatured form. Wilde, however, inserts some sly references that has Lady Bracknell depict herself, unashamedly and unironically, as the upstart social climber, the Mrs Erlynne who has fossilized into her role after twenty years: 'When I married Lord Bracknell I had no fortune of any kind. But I never dreamed for a moment of allowing that to stand in my way.'[63]

In her hypocrisy, moral flexibility and essential absurdity, Lady Bracknell *is* Society, the same one that imposed the rigid stereotype in Wilde's previous comedies and the one which the characters in *The Importance of Being Earnest* gleefully subvert. Lady Bracknell's stereotypes here, however, are absurd only because they eventually backfire: Jack acquires parents and one of them is her sister and she hastily reconsiders Cecily's eligibility upon learning of her fortune. But Lady Bracknell's great comedic talent is that she remains

62 Ibid., 267.

63 Ibid., 299–300. The most memorable performance of Lady Bracknell is still Dame Edith Evans's portrayal as the immortal dragon in the 1938 Globe Theatre production of *The Importance of Being Earnest* which she later revived in Anthony Asquith's 1952 film. (Coincidentally, Evans also portrayed Lady Wishfort in a 1923 theatrical production of *The Way of the World*.) Dame Judi Dench's more sexualized 1983 performance of Lady Bracknell for the Royal National Theatre Company was notable in that this Lady Bracknell was a former showgirl who married up; the class-crossing and golddigging implications were revisited in Oliver Parker's 2002 film adaptation, also co-starring Dench as Lady Bracknell.

oblivious to these nuances. Like the society which Wilde criticizes relentlessly in his comedies, she trundles on in her absurdity, changing too slowly for people's liking, and, like the division into acts, the stock characters or the externally-driven plot device, structuring the dramatic conflicts of both the theatre and of everyday life.

Chapter Six
Performance as Redemption in *De Profundis* and *The Ballad of Reading Gaol*

Although while writing this study I have been concerned primarily with the development of Wilde's theory of performance as a cultural and literary theory, it has been impossible not to notice the second narrative embedded in Wilde's theory. That is, as he is writing about performance, and especially about persona, his own public persona becomes more and more of a structuring agent for how his writings are received and read. Wilde's focus on his own image, his brilliantly insouciant statements and his carefully cultivated friendships with celebrities made his own public persona a collaboration with the press, a collaboration about which he was always ambivalent. Writers like Ellmann and Gagnier have always maintained that Wilde courted the press' attention enthusiastically, that he maintained control of his public persona and that he was able to manipulate even the less-flattering public portrayals of him. Other critics have followed this interpretation of Wilde in order to challenge another interpretation which sees him as both victim and martyr. Given this portrait of Wilde as a player in the celebrity game, however, it can be difficult to reconcile it with the idea of Wilde as a sincere, non-campy thinker who was using his writings to describe what he saw as an important mode of creation and interpretation in both the individual and in late-Victorian culture.

However, both of these ideas – persona as a cultural hermeneutic and persona as insertion into the cultural marketplace, as sincere intellectual endeavour and as ironic manipulation – coexist, if sometimes uncomfortably, within the course of Wilde's life as a writer. It is a serendipitous example of Wilde's contention in 'The Critic as Artist' that the individual is fragmented and multiple and that 'realizing one's self fully' consists of performing the paradoxes inherent in one's own character. But the press' depiction of Wilde only overshadows his writings twice and both times Wilde also has to contend with its wilful misunderstandings of his writings and ideas. The first time occurs at the beginning of Wilde's celebrity, the period of his friendships with famous actresses and his lectures, when he was caricatured as the representative of the Aesthetic Movement. The second time occurs during what would romantically be labelled later as Wilde's fall, the period of his sentencing and imprisonment for gross indecency. Interestingly, the press' enthusiastic return to mocking Wilde in 1895 uses the same caricatures and tropes it did in the early 1880s, returning triumphantly to the old stereotypes of Wilde as the foppish aesthete, only this time as more of a monstrous than a ridiculous figure.

Influenced by Hegelian thinking, Wilde saw persona as a dialectic without a synthesis (except possibly for his utopian vision in 'The Soul of Man under Socialism'), a struggle between the artist's desire to use his or her own persona as the performance of an individuated self and the public's desire to use it as a commodity, whether to sell ice cream or cigars or to insist it be performed as a particular 'type' for ideological purposes. His writings were parables of the individual struggling to keep his or her persona away from the manipulations of Philistine society, and the Philistines Wilde had direct experience with were the ideologically conservative writers and artists of the mainstream press. He gives his most trenchant criticism of the press to Mrs. Cheveley as her threat to Sir Robert:

> Suppose that when I leave this house I drive down to some newspaper office, and give them this scandal and the proofs of it. Think of their loathsome joy, of the delight they would have in dragging you down, of the mud and mire they would plunge you in. Think of the hypocrite with his greasy

> smile penning his leading article, and arranging the foulness of the public placard.[1]

Mrs. Cheveley's description could easily be a description of some later stage of Dorian Gray's picture; her speech points to sensational newspaper stories, of exaggerated caricatures and portraits meant to camouflage the repressed desires of the hypocritical writers. It is similar to the exchange of desires Wilde discusses in 'The Portrait of Mr. W.H.'; the difference here is that the press' desires are perverted by the Philistine ideology it is invested in.

And it would seem that Wilde's views about the press were accurate. In March 1895, when Wilde sued the Marquess of Queensberry for libel, on account of Queensberry having sent Wilde a note accusing him of 'posing as a somdomite [*sic*],' he found that the press reacted in a manner quite similar to Mrs. Cheveley's dark predictions. Despite the transformations in Wilde's public persona since the early 1880s from the aesthete to the urbane playwright, the earlier persona had the most symbolic resonance to the press when journalists began to write stories about his trials; certainly it provided reporters with more outlandish and sensationalist descriptions. An article in *The Evening News* on 9 March 1895, the first day of the Queensberry hearing preceding the first of the trials, depicted Wilde driving up 'in a carriage and pair, a magnificent turn-out with coachman and cockaded footman' and described how he took the oath with aesthetic grace.'[2] A headline from *The Star* on 3 April 1895, the first day of the trial against Queensberry, could easily have been lifted from an article about Wilde's lectures almost fifteen years before: 'The Aesthete Gives Characteristically Cynical Evidence, Replete with Painted Epigram and Startling Paradox, and Explains His Views on Morality in Art.'[3] Granted, both of these newspapers were basically

---

1 Wilde, *An Ideal Husband*, 181.

2 *The Evening News*, 9 March 1895.

3 *The Star*, 3 April 1895.

entertainment publications and looked to sensationalize their stories whenever possible. But even though Wilde had stopped performing as the aesthete by the mid-1880s, the press in returning to this early persona endeavoured, as it did in the early 1880s, to make Wilde look both sexually menacing and ridiculous, and to depict the trial as the moral consequence of Wilde's posturing.

As a result of the trial, or more specifically of the alleged libel which caused Wilde to sue Queensberry in the first place, the newspaper references to Wilde the aesthete were thinly-veiled allusions to him 'posing as a somdomite [*sic*].' When Queensberry was acquitted and Wilde arraigned on charges of gross indecency, the tenor of the articles shifted from portraying Wilde as an aging version of the foppish aesthete to a more vulgar, grotesque figure of a sexual deviant. The *Star* article which began with the headline reminiscent of a *Punch* cartoon also described Wilde as 'ponderous and fleshy.'[4] As the first of Wilde's three trials progressed, the newspaper accounts of him became more accusatory. When Wilde was charged with gross indecency on 6 April 1895, the press took a twofold approach to maligning his character. In one approach, the newspapers described Wilde in terms reminiscent of Jekyll and Hyde, trying to link him in the public imagination to the monster Hyde and to the Whitechapel murders of 1888. The barbed repartee between Wilde and Edward Carson, the Crown Prosecutor, where Wilde outwitted Carson during the interrogation of *The Picture of Dorian Gray*, was followed by Carson questioning Wilde about his sexual exploits with young male prostitutes. As suggested by *The Evening News* in an article on 5 April 1895, Wilde's sophisticated persona was a mask hiding his moral degradation and his eagerness to troll lower-class areas:

---

4 Ibid.

> The fine verbal fencing of the first day has done little to relieve the horrible darkness of the succeeding passages of this trial, and even the Old Bailey recoiled with loathing from the long ordeal of terrible suggestion that occupied the whole of yesterday when the cross-examination left the artistic literary plane and entered the dim-lit, perfumed rooms where the poet of the beautiful joined with valets and grooms in the bond of the silver cigarette case. And when Oscar Wilde left the box the little light that had relieved the awful sombreness of the picture died out, as Mr. Carson went on to paint a horrid nocturne of terrible suggestions, a thing of blackness, only half defined, but wholly horrible.[5]

The newspapers began to reread Wilde's writings as unambiguous evidence of his homosexuality. As Alan Sinfield has pointed out, Wilde's trials were the occasion that led to a widespread equation of his style with queer style and to the use of his name as a queer signifier.[6] The *Daily Telegraph* of 6 April 1895 proclaimed:

> We shall have purchased the pain and shame of such an exhibition at a price, perhaps not too high if it lead the youth of our generation, on the one hand, to graver thoughts of duty and propriety, and the public, on the other, to a sterner impatience with those who, under the name of Art, or some other pretence, insidiously poison our stage our literature, our drama, and the outskirts of our press.[7]

(The *Daily Telegraph* fancied itself a much more serious newspaper than its tabloid counterparts.)

What resulted from the trials in terms of Wilde's persona was that it became fixed as an image of sexual perversion by the conservative members of the press and as an image of the fallen man by more sympathetic journalists. For instance, on the day of Wilde's conviction, the *London Evening News* ran an editorial stating that

---

5 *The Evening News*, 5 April 1895.

6 Sinfield, *The Wilde Century*.

7 *The Daily Telegraph*, 6 April 1895.

> England has tolerated the man Wilde and others of his kind too long. Before he broke the law of his country and outraged human decency he was a social pest, a centre of intellectual corruption. He was one of the high priests of a school which attacks all the wholesome, manly, simple ideals of English life, and sets up false gods of decadent culture and intellectual debauchery. The man himself was a perfect type of his class, a gross sensualist veneered with the affectation of artistic feeling too delicate for the appreciation of common clay. To him and such as him we owe the spread of moral degeneration amongst young men with abilities sufficient to make them a credit to their country.[8]

Wilde in this editorial became more than type; he became a symptom for a growing anxiety about the health and vigour of England's youth. Whereas the earliest caricatures of Wilde portrayed him as a potential sexual threat to England's youth, the *London Evening News*' editorial baldly portrayed Wilde as a threat to the masculinity of English boys, a masculinity which it explicitly linked to nationalism. Wilde also became a representative of the homosexual predator and this description transformed his persona in its entirety. Although previously the press blamed all of his behaviour and pronouncements on his aestheticism, by the end of the trials Wilde's entire persona was seen as being symptomatic of a sexual perversion. As Ed Cohen points out, since the press was prohibited from naming the crimes that first Queensberry, then the Crown, accused Wilde of committing, it could only convey these crimes indirectly by transforming the entirety of Wilde's persona into a sexual deviant.[9] The image of Wilde then became a sign for a type of individual, and by extension a series of sexual behaviours, which previously had no way of being named in public.[10]

---

8 *London Evening News*, 25 May 1895.

9 Ed Cohen, *Talk on the Wilde Side: Toward a Genealogy of a Discourse on Male Sexualities* (New York: Routledge, 1993), 146.

10 It is a sad irony that Wilde, in detailing the struggle between the individual persona and the will of society to stereotype, would find himself having lost the struggle during the course of the trials.

Even the more sympathetic papers, such as *The Illustrated Police Budget* (another tabloid publication) concentrated on a sensational, melodramatic portrayal of Wilde stripped of his identity. Reporting on Wilde's first night at the Bow Street Police Station, the newspaper focused on Wilde's meticulous toilet, emphasizing the pitiable incongruity between the fashionable gentleman he once was and the abject criminal he has now become.[11] When Wilde was sentenced to two years' imprisonment with hard labour, *The Illustrated Police Budget* again concentrated on the loss of Wilde's public image:

> The prison barber, who is a man well used to his work, at once commenced to crop off with a pair of scissors Oscar's renowned and ever admired – at least by Society – locks. It must have taken Mr. Wilde years to train and grow his hair as it stood early on Saturday; it took the prison barber just two minutes to cut all the locks off.[12]

Wilde is reconstructed as a tragic Samson figure, his hair a synecdoche for his fame and public persona. The article in effect transforms him from an artist to a character trapped within a persona not of his own making.

De Profundis, Wilde's letter to Lord Alfred Douglas, was written during his incarceration in Reading Prison, the last of three prisons in which he served his sentence, and it was written following a particularly upsetting crisis over his public persona. While at Reading, Wilde made several unsuccessful efforts to convince the English government to reduce his sentence. In order to do so, he invoked the image the public had of him as a sexual deviant. In a letter to the Home Secretary on 2 July 1896, Wilde appealed for an early release, arguing that he was suffering from a form of 'sexual madness' which was considered a sickness, not a crime, in several other European countries. He asked for an increase in his allotment of books, claiming that

11 *The Illustrated Police Budget*, 13 April 1895.

12 *The Illustrated Police Budget*, 1 June 1895.

idleness might lead him to dwell upon his sexual vices. He cited the works of Italian criminologist Cesare Lombroso and Lombroso's disciple Max Nordau as experts who had made a scientific

> connection between madness and the literary and artistic temperament. Professor Nordau in his book on 'Degenerescence' [*sic*] published in 1894 having devoted an entire chapter to the petitioner as a specially typical example of this fatal law.[13]

Wilde continued his appeal to the Home Secretary, elaborating upon his 'madness' in another letter written on 10 November 1896:

> Of all the modes of insanity – and the petitioner is fully conscious now, too conscious it may be, that his whole life, for the two years preceding his ruin, was the prey of absolute madness – the insanity of perverted sensual instinct is the one most dominant in its action on the brain.[14]

It is difficult to gauge with what degree of sincerity Wilde wrote those humiliating letters. Certainly it is tempting to imagine an unrepentant Wilde who donned the pose of the penitent, fully aware of both its exigency and its artificiality. On the other hand, many Wilde biographers have organized his life into a parable of the Fall and in this case the sincere penitent would be the more appropriate performance. It would likely be more accurate to suggest that Wilde was aware of the artificiality of this performance but was nonetheless sincere in his use of it. Prison amounted to a near-complete destruction of Wilde's artistic persona, largely because it deprived him of the material conditions necessary to cultivate it. The newspapers and general public were calling him a pervert and a monster. He was forbidden to communicate with other prisoners. The letters

---

13 Wilde, *Complete Letters*, 656. Wilde was denied his petition, but the Home Secretary did increase his supply of books.

14 Ibid., 667. In this letter, Wilde again asked to be released from prison, but this petition was also denied.

he was permitted to write were limited in number as well as heavily censored, his reading was restricted, and he was subjected to a strict schedule which included punishing, repetitive labour such as picking oakum and walking on an inclined treadmill six hours a day.[15] By the time Wilde arrived at Reading Prison, he was so weakened by the hard labour as well as by a fall that damaged his ear, that he was assigned light gardening duties and acted as a makeshift librarian, delivering books to other convicts.[16]

In 1905, when he included an abridged version for the first collected works of Wilde's writings, Sir Robert Ross titled Wilde's long letter to Douglas *De Profundis*, or 'Out of the Depths,' which is an accurate name for the persona Wilde ended up cultivating (and, appropriately, also the name of a prayer taken from Psalm 129, known in the Catholic faith as one of the penitential Psalms). In this letter, Wilde refashioned himself as abject, suffering, and the modern-day Wandering Jew, but to do any refashioning at all constituted an act of defiance against the public's typing of him as a sexual monster and of other people's intent to exploit this new persona. Among those whom Wilde felt were taking unfair advantage of his disgrace was Lord Alfred Douglas and it is likely that in his letter Wilde put a disproportionate emphasis on his volatile relationship with Douglas. But while he was being held at Holloway Prison during his trials, Wilde wrote some love letters to Douglas; some weeks later, when he was petitioning the Home Secretary for early release in order to prevent his relapse into 'erotomania,'[17] he learned that Douglas was planning to publish an article about his relationship with Wilde in the *Mercure de France*, a Paris newspaper which had fervently denounced Wilde during his trials. Douglas had planned to

15 Regenia Gagnier, '*De Profundis* as *Epistola: in Carcere et Vinculis*: A Materialist Reading of Oscar Wilde's Autobiography.' *Criticism* 26, no. 4 (1984), 335–354.

16 Ellmann, *Oscar Wilde*, 496.

17 Wilde, *Complete Letters*, 657.

include several of the love letters in the article and Wilde from prison had pleaded with Ross to stop Douglas from printing this article. Referring to him as 'Douglas' rather than by the endearment 'Bosie,' Wilde wrote to Ross:

> The idea that he is wearing or in possession of anything I gave him is peculiarly repugnant to me. I cannot of course get rid of the revolting memories of the two years I was unlucky enough to have him with me, or of the mode by which he thrust me into the abyss of ruin and disgrace to gratify his hatred of his father and other ignoble passions.[18]

For Wilde, a persona is an instance of agency only if it is engaged in some sort of dialogue or dialectic, whether ultimately supportive, such as the relationships which develop out of mutual attraction and influence, or agonistic, such as the dialectic between the individual and the societal. In refashioning his persona, Wilde needed an antithetical voice to help structure his development of it. The collective late-Victorian voice, represented by the 'loathsome, hypocritical' press, was at that point too powerful and totalizing to be a worthy antagonist – Wilde was aware, as he later writes in *The Ballad of Reading Gaol*, of society's hypocritical stance towards his 'crimes' and 'vices' but also had to concede society's current victory over him. Douglas, in his obliviousness, his upper-class status, his general lack of maturity and depth, provided Wilde with the perfect reflection of society's shortcomings and thus became the catalyst in *De Profundis* for Wilde's development of a new persona.

Wilde wrote to his friend More Adey on 18 February 1897,

> I told you I was going to write to Alfred Douglas. I am still at work on the letter. It is the most important letter of my life, as it will deal ultimately with my future mental attitude towards life, with the way in which I desire to meet

18 Ibid., 655.

the world again, with the development of my character: with what I have lost, what I have learned, and what I hope to arrive at.[19]

De Profundis was intended to be Wilde's manifesto of his new persona; chastising Douglas provided him with the reason to write it. Previously, Wilde had written a letter to Ross where he enumerated Douglas' faults and this list of complaints became the beginning of the longer draft. Douglas had become to Wilde the reason for his ruin; therefore Douglas would be the image around which Wilde would rebuild himself.

Wilde's intended title for the letter was 'Epistola: In Carcere et Vinculis,' or 'Letter: Imprisoned and Chained,' and Wilde, evoking his character The Happy Prince, connects his confining relationship with Douglas, pleasurable though it was at times, to his current state of imprisonment. The letter is as much an open letter to the public that condemned him as a criminal as it is specifically addressed to Douglas and more importantly it is less a letter than a narrative of Wilde's redemption and reclaiming of his persona. In fact, *De Profundis* reiterates a familiar narrative pattern in Wilde's fairy tales and short stories: the abject sufferer finds redemption and beauty by transforming his suffering into acts of compassion. This pattern is present in the aforementioned 'The Happy Prince,' for example. The Prince, who has lived his life trapped behind the walls of the palace *Sans Souci*, is turned into a beautiful statue after his death. Unable to bear the sufferings of the city's poor, he has his companion, a Swallow, strip him of his jewels and gold leaf in order to provide solace to some of the poorer of the city's inhabitants. After the Prince has stripped away all of his external adornments, he and the Swallow are disposed of as trash by the city magistrates but are then plucked by God's angels out of the rubbish fire to dwell in Paradise. In another fairy tale, 'The Young King,' the eponymous

19 Ibid., 678.

hero is discovered living among shepherds as a child and is taken to an aesthetically-designed palace to begin his reign. In a series of Joseph-like dreams, he learns that his coronation finery comes from the suffering of the workers and therefore refuses to wear either the robe, crown, or sceptre, arriving at his coronation in his shepherd's rags. After listening to the jeers of his courtiers and subjects, a light in the church surrounds his head like a nimbus and causes his wooden staff to blossom.

In *De Profundis*, Wilde depicts himself as having been stripped of all of his external finery – in this case, of his position in society and of his persona as an artist – and is searching for a means to rebuild his persona out of his suffering. For Wilde, the disappearance of his former persona corresponds to the disappearance of the material aspects of his identity. As he mentions at different points throughout the letter, his wife, children, friends, reputation, career, income, and even name have been taken away from him. In addition, while in prison he suffered the humiliation of those letters he wrote to the Home Secretary as well as being informed that, because of his unpaid court costs and the bankruptcy that followed, his nemesis Queensberry now had claim to any publication or production royalties. This process of denuding his identity gives Wilde the analogy to Jokanaan, for baptism and rebirth in the form of the second part of *De Profundis*. He therefore uses this letter to be both personally repentant, especially in his regret over the pain he caused his family and his fall from grace as an artist, and socially unrepentant; as Jay Losey suggests: 'Wilde wants his future readers to regard him as an artist who remained socially impenitent while acknowledging his personal shortcomings.'[20]

The Lord Alfred Douglas depicted in *De Profundis* is constructed in a particular way in order to position him as Wilde's antagonist. As

20 Jay Losey, 'The Aesthetics of Exile: Wilde Transforming Dante in *Intentions* and *De Profundis*.' *ELT* 36, no. 4 (1993), 446.

William E. Buckler notes, Wilde's perception in 1897 of his past actions were heavily influenced by the outcome of his trials and, with *De Profundis*, he 'is involved in a process of myth-making, converting personal history into personalized fable.'[21] For instance, despite his claims that Douglas inhibited his creativity, Wilde wrote *Salome* and all of his social comedies during their relationship. Despite his charge of Douglas leading him into sexual peccadilloes, Wilde often conducted his affairs with younger men independently of Douglas. As Regenia Gagnier notes,

> If there had not been an Alfred Douglas, Wilde would have had to invent one. Douglas was for Wilde the image of all unworthy audiences: once he was demystified he could be forgiven, and Wilde could go on to demystify and forgive the whole society he had played to.[22]

While Wilde's grievances against Douglas were sincere (Douglas, after all, is rarely seen by Wilde biographers in flattering terms), the faithless, shallow lover in *De Profundis* is set up as a straw man. Under the conceit of attempting to re-educate him, Wilde can put forth the principles that he intends will shape his new persona.

Douglas' persona of the beautiful but spoiled and petulant boy is frequently positioned in *De Profundis* against Wilde's abject persona. To further his point, Wilde asserts that Douglas' persona, rather than being based on Art, is instead based on artifice, a shallow and frivolous corruption of Art, thus returning to his argument in *The Picture of Dorian Gray*. The example Wilde gives to support this assertion is a particular incident that occurred while he was in Holloway Prison. Douglas, in Paris at the time, had managed to pass a surreptitious message to him through a friend who was visiting Wilde. The alias he used was a nickname Wilde had once given him:

---

21 William E. Buckler, 'Oscar Wilde's Aesthetic of the Self: Art as Imaginative Self-Realization in *De Profundis*.' *Biography* 12, no. 2 (1989), 96, 102.

22 Gagnier, *Idylls of the Marketplace*, 180.

'Prince Fleur-de-Lys.' Wilde's indignation about this incident stems from the name itself; the reference to artifice and luxury mocked his current situation and the aesthetic connotations indirectly referred to the press' misusing of Wilde's aesthetic persona as a symbol of his perversion. Wilde then uses this incident to paint Douglas as shallow and misguided in his performance:

> You were in your own eyes still the graceful prince of a trivial comedy, not the sombre figure of a tragic show. All that had occurred was but a feather for the cap that gilds a narrow head, a flower to pink the doublet that hides a heart that Hate, and Hate alone, can warm, that Love, and Love alone, finds cold.[23]

Wilde accuses Douglas of basic insensitivity here; he performs but does not understand the inappropriateness of his performance. But Douglas' main sin, according to Wilde, is his inability to alter his performance; despite his lover's suffering, Douglas remains light-hearted and acts immaturely. And Wilde sustains this accusation throughout *De Profundis*, accusing Douglas of disturbing, if not outright destroying, Wilde's relationship with his art.

Wilde's obsession with Douglas' misbehaviours – his temper tantrums, his overspending, his irrational hatred of his father – is not only Wilde airing his resentment after months of incarceration. Through this extremely unflattering portrayal, Douglas' persona in this letter becomes the representation of the Philistine society that in Wilde's view punished him for being an artist. It is therefore through the education of Douglas that Wilde can reconstruct his persona and through teaching Douglas to embrace Wilde's new abject persona that Wilde can be socially redeemed. Wilde's writing in *De Profundis* is purposely didactic at times in order to convert Douglas from callowness into maturity, or into sympathy with Wilde's suffering. Addressing Douglas directly, he writes: 'Is it be-

23 Oscar Wilde, *De Profundis*, in *The Complete Letters of Oscar* Wilde, ed. Merlin Holland and Rupert Hart-Davis, 683–780 (New York: Henry Holt, 2000), 716–717.

ginning to dawn on you what Love is, and what is the nature of Love? It is not too late for you to learn, though to teach it to you I may have had to go to a convict's cell.'[24]

In cultivating his new persona, Wilde uses suffering as his new paradigm, exploring the nature of suffering as a way to learn about the self in isolation and to engage completely in an ideal community of fellow-sufferers, the ideal of which is his description of Christ. It is a paradoxical stance, since the outcast (as Wilde portrays himself) is in *De Profundis* both a liminal figure and a fully-engaged participant in communitas but it is the necessary first step in Wilde's reconstruction of himself. Communitas is largely made up of downtrodden, marginalized groups, often victims of the enforcement of social norms, and Turner argues that communitas is a way of interacting outside of constricting social roles: 'People have a real need . . .to doff the masks, cloaks, apparel, and insignia of status from time to time even if only to don the liberating masks of liminal masquerade.'[25] Wilde's communitas of fellow prisoners comes to its full fruition in *The Ballad of Reading Gaol*; here, his notion of the outcast is the revolutionary individualist whom he first introduced in 'The Soul of Man under Socialism.' The performance of the outcast leads to individualism, whose epitome is Wilde's concept of Christ, which eventually leads to a communitas subverting the social order.

In *De Profundis*, Wilde connects his suffering to the law. He makes it clear in several instances that his suffering is not the suffering of remorse; rather, it is an external affliction, brought upon him by a narrow-minded society and an overly-punitive legal system. 'Reason does not help me,' he writes. 'It tells me that the laws under which I am convicted are wrong and unjust laws, and the system under which I have suffered a wrong and unjust system.'[26] The

24 Ibid., 715.

25 Turner, *Dramas, Fields, and Metaphors*, 243.

26 Wilde, *De Profundis*, 732.

structure of the law can only be criticized successfully by the social outcast, particularly the social outcast as artist. Wilde fashions himself in *De Profundis* as the Romantic Wandering Jew, the Melmoth whose name he adopts upon release from prison, as an artistic standpoint. With his persona as an artist, Wilde's suffering becomes a catalyst for social criticism; with his persona as an outcast, his suffering becomes a catalyst for his art:

> It will force on me the necessity of again asserting myself as an artist, and as soon as I possibly can. If I can produce even one more beautiful work of art I shall be able to rob malice of its venom, and cowardice of its sneer, and to pluck out the tongue of scorn by the roots.[27]

Norbert Kohl explains, 'No humble, uncomplaining resignation to his fate, but instead its aesthetic elevation to the scale of an historic drama – this was how Wilde was able to adapt himself to his new situation.'[28] The historic drama culminates in artistic transubstantiation, as Wilde introduces Christ as his new ego ideal. The Christ of *De Profundis* is the human Christ of Renan's *Life of Jesus* (*Vie de Jésus*), a book which Wilde read in prison. Renan portrays a Christ whose deification is a result of others' perceptions of him, a modern Christ who reflects the nineteenth century's interest in taxonomies of the visual.[29] The parallels between Renan's Christ and Wilde's self-portrait in *De Profundis* are striking; not only does Renan portray Christ as a nexus of other people's desires, but his Christ also becomes more isolated as he grows in influence. For Wilde, Christ represents the transformation into sheer performance, persona in its essence: 'He is just like a work of art himself. He does not really teach one anything, but by being brought into his presence one

---

27 Ibid., 734.

28 Kohl, *Oscar Wilde*, 286.

29 Ernest Renan, *The Life of Jesus* (London: Watts and Co., 1861).

becomes something.'[30] Like the influential personalities of 'The Portrait of Mr. W.H.' or *The Picture of Dorian Gray*, Christ's mode of being is fascinating enough to instigate change in his audience. Wilde, fearing his exile from the British stage and possibly from all walks of literature, is positing a less worldly, more isolated stance from which to perform, but it is a stance that, in contradiction to Renan's work and his own previous writings, does not need exposure to others to develop his performance.

The Christ of *De Profundis*, as Guy Willoughby points out, is a model of 'daunting achievement of self-perfection through absolute individualism.'[31] Wilde's description of Christ repeatedly links art with suffering, stating at the end that suffering is a catalyst for a greater type of art. 'And feeling,' he writes,

> with the artistic nature of one to whom Sorrow and Suffering were modes through which [Christ] could realise his conception of the Beautiful, that an idea is of no value till it becomes incarnate and is made an image, he makes of himself the image of the Man of Sorrows, and as such has fascinated and dominated Art as no Greek god ever succeeded in doing.[32]

In suffering, Wilde ultimately finds the means to recover his individuality, a paradoxical move from the man who previously claimed that suffering was the thing that made men indistinguishable from one another in prison. But, through his writing about suffering, Wilde, as Joseph Butwin points out, 'becomes for himself the playwright, the player, and the audience or, in comparable mercantile terms, the publicist, the product, and the consumer.'[33] In other words, by portraying himself as the suffering outcast, he separates

30 Wilde, *De Profundis*, 753.

31 Guy Willoughby, *Art and Christhood: The Aesthetics of Oscar Wilde* (Cranbury, N.J.: Associated Univ. Press, 1993), 107.

32 Wilde, *De Profundis*, 746.

33 Joseph Butwin, 'The Martyr Clown: Oscar Wilde in *De Profundis*.' *Victorian Newsletter* 42 (1972), 2.

himself from society; by doing so, he regains control over his own persona.

In order to develop his new persona as a suffering outcast, Wilde makes the press' construction of him as a sexual monster the touchstone of his transformation. 'I would sooner say, or hear it said of me,' he writes,

> that I was so typical a child of my age that in my perversity, and for that perversity's sake, I turned the good things of my life to evil, and the evil things of my life to good. What is said, however, by myself or by others matters little. The important thing, the thing that lies before me, the thing that I have to do, or be the brief remainder of my days one maimed, marred, and incomplete, is to absorb into my nature all that has been done to me, to make it part of me, to accept it without complaint, fear, or reluctance.[34]

By absorbing his sexual 'crimes,' his artistic principles and his sense of suffering into one persona, Wilde transforms himself into a cautionary symbol of a very different sort, one which warns society that it creates the monsters it desires. He positions himself as a martyr, not to his sexuality, but to his theory of performance and to his conviction that the development of the self along artistic lines is a socially ameliorative act.

By the time Wilde wrote *De Profundis*, he saw his persona as the one construct he could use to rebuild his shattered reputation and identity. The fact that he could manipulate his idea of persona in such a way demonstrates how far his theories of performance and persona had come from the intellectual fancy at Oxford to the conviction that persona can be developed as social criticism. Wilde saw in his ideas about persona a fundamental connection between aestheticism and experience, one which could be realized in a variety of performances, from textual performance to the performance of everyday life. He championed the potential for a persona to liberate

34 Wilde, *De Profundis*, 732–733.

the individual from the pressure to conform to social expectations, seeing in a persona an individual's capability to become a living work of art.

The Ballad of Reading Gaol, Wilde's last completed work, was written shortly after his release from prison in 1897. The poem, which Wilde admitted was fragmented, skirts between a gritty, naturalistic depiction of prison life; an allegorical tale reminiscent of Coleridge's *Rime of the Ancient Mariner*, Dante's *Inferno*, and Wilde's own fairy tales; and a religious poem that elaborates on Wilde's conception of Christ in *De Profundis*. In compiling the *Oxford Book of Modern Verse* for its 1936 publication, Yeats cut out the parts of the poem that were not 'documentary' in nature and Ellmann's assessment of the poem succinctly sums up the views of many in the scholarly community: 'The *Ballad* is strongest when it concentrates on the trooper and prison conditions, weakest when it deals with capitalized abstractions like Sin and Death.'[35] It is this very disjuncture, however, that makes the *Ballad* possibly Wilde's most trenchant and incisive writing about performance for it is a poem that quite blatantly assumes performance to be the way in which people are called forth as social beings. In this poem the artistic 'persona' has been superseded by compulsive performance; the punishment for these criminals is the negation of their own subjective agency.

The Ballad of Reading Gaol is a poem about the construction of the criminal's persona, both as public scapegoat and as private negation of one's previous self, and its creation out of the mandated performances which make up prison life. The main character of the poem is based on Charles Woolridge, a soldier who was incarcerated in Reading Gaol for murdering his wife and who was serving his sentence at the same time as Wilde.[36] Rather than a traditional

35 Ellmann, *Oscar Wilde*, 533.

36 The image of the murder taking place in the marriage bed, however, is an invention of Wilde's.

narrative character, Wilde creates a single image of a man walking in a circle in the prison yard, in the drab greys of a prison uniform (which Wilde contrasts sharply to the red of his army uniform), doing nothing but looking wistfully at the sky. For all the critical commentary that this character is supposed to represent a Christlike sacrificial figure, stoically carrying the weight of everyone's sins, his primary function in the poem is to be watched by others – the prisoners, the guards, and even, by revisiting this recurring image throughout the poem, the reader.

The condemned man exists as an *ur*-text for every crime and peccadillo imagined, not by the narrator or the other prisoners who are never fleshed out sufficiently to warrant such complex interior thoughts, but by the reader. He bears the mark of a crime of passion by Wilde explicitly linking his red uniform to the blood, wine and the 'poor dead woman' but he also displays the educative intents of prison life.[37] The suit of shabby grey that he wears and the leeching of all passion and life from his expression represent the prison's intent to recreate this man into the prisoner, a specific type whose sins efface his individuality. Colours play an important part in the first section of the poem – the red of the condemned man's crime plays against the lifeless grey of his prison uniform and the blue of the sky which, in contrast to the dull colours of prison life, promises rescue and salvation from the excruciating conditions of the gaol. Wilde is treating these colours as allegorical stage and costume design, which he borrowed from his experiences with the staging of his own plays. Red is the colour of passion and, to Wilde, who adopts this idea from the conclusion of *The Renaissance*, passion is the desire for experience and for realizing one's personality. Grey, on the other hand, recreates the man as a criminal by depriving him literally of any other colour. He is the object on which society can impose its characterization of

37 Oscar Wilde, *The Ballad of Reading Gaol*, in *The Complete Works of Oscar Wilde*, 843–860 (New York: Barnes and Noble, 1994), 843.

the delinquent individual. As Foucault notes in *Discipline and Punish*, the prisoner as a type 'isolates, outlines, brings out a form of illegality that seems to sum up symbolically all the others, but which makes it possible to leave in the shade those that one wishes to – or must – tolerate.'[38] The great punishment of prison life, according to Wilde, is the negation of all individualizing characteristics, and society's victory in transforming an individual into a type.

The condemned man's aimless, circular walk gives us a particular kind of performing act, one that Wilde uses to illustrate the poem's famous line: 'Each man kills the thing he loves,'[39] itself a reworking of Bassanio's question in *The Merchant of Venice*: 'Do all men kill the things they do not love?' The line and the examples that Wilde gives in its support are illustrative of a way of being that mimics imprisonment. Strangling 'with the hands of Lust' or 'with the hands of Gold'[40] places these implied criminals into a decadent social order; sexuality and economic progress turn in on themselves and lead to death rather than to forward movement. Wilde's conception of human relationships that are intertwined with human destruction presages Antonio Gramsci's assertion that the bourgeois state eventually becomes 'saturated,' that 'it not only does not expand – it starts to disintegrate.'[41] This is an important statement for Wilde in terms of his view of English society; the compulsive heterosexuality that condemned him in the first place likened his homoerotic attractions to a degenerate, disintegrate form of human relationship. As Kevin Kopelson remarks, while in prison Wilde begins to write about homoeroticism as 'figur[ing] itself in terms of

---

38 Michel Foucault, *Discipline and Punish: The Birth of the Prison*, trans. Alan Sheridan (New York: Vintage, 1995), 276.

39 Wilde, *The Ballad of Reading Gaol*, 844.

40 Ibid.

41 Antonio Gramsci, *Selections from the Prison Notebooks*, ed. and trans. Quintin Hoare and Geoffrey Nowell Smith (London: Lawrence and Wishart, 1971), 260.

self-contained murderous energies'[42] and this is borne out not only in *De Profundis* but in the humiliating letters Wilde writes to the Home Secretary. In rewriting this condemning concept of homoeroticism into heterosexuality with the use of the words 'each man,' the direct evocation of a man's murder of a woman, and the prisoner's endless circular walking, Wilde throughout the poem argues for the arbitrariness and essential hypocrisy of both the English judicial system and the compulsive heterosexuality upon which many of the laws are structured. It is a dangerous claim that he makes; critics have rightly noted that Wilde runs the risk of trivializing murder.[43] But it is the prison system of the late nineteenth century which makes no distinction between murderers, homosexuals, and even young children. Wilde, for his crime of gross indecency, is sentenced to the same place as Woolridge and he writes, both in his poem and in a letter to the *Daily Chronicle* arguing for prison reforms, about a crying child in a nearby cell.[44]

Wilde figures this perceived arbitrariness as a performance; specifically he claims in the poem that the prisoners' performances are structured so that they externalize society's own repressed self-hatred. Foucault writes that the prison system which predates the one of Wilde's time figured the prisoners' very bodies as texts so that bystanders would procure some kind of knowledge by reading their abject bodies.[45] It becomes an interesting phenomenon in Wilde's poem – in a closed prison system, there is still a mandated

---

42 Kevin R. Kopelson. 'Wilde's Love-Deaths.' *Yale Journal of Criticism* 5, no. 3 (1992), 44.

43 Leonard Nathan, 'The Ballads of Reading Gaol: At the Limits of the Lyric,' in *Critical Essays on Oscar Wilde*, ed. Regenia Gagnier, 213–222 (New York: G.K. Hall, 1991), 217. See also Karen Alkalay-Gut, 'The Thing He Loves: Murder as Aesthetic Experience in The Ballad of Reading Gaol.' *Victorian Poetry* 35, no. 3 (1997), 352.

44 Wilde, *Complete Letters*, 849.

45 Foucault, *Discipline and Punish*, 43.

costume, series of tasks and movements, and specific roles played by prison guards and doctors. The chaplain 'robed in white,' the sherriff 'stern with gloom' and the governor 'all in shiny black, / With the yellow face of Doom'[46] are described as macabre characters according to allegorical theatrical conventions; it is their costumes and mask-like expressions which convey their characters. In this performance, the performers are also the spectators, hence the emphasis Wilde places on watching. The prisoners watch the condemned man 'with gaze of dull amaze'[47] and Wilde describes the condemned man as constantly being accompanied by two vigilant warders:

> Or else he sat with those who watched
> His anguish night and day;
> Who watched him when he rose to weep,
> And when he crouched to pray;
> Who watched him lest himself should rob
> Their scaffold of its prey.[48]

The watching in this case is preventative; Wilde figures the upcoming execution as a performance, or even a ritual, that must be completed. The condemned man is not sentenced to death, but to participation in the performance of his own execution. As both Foucault and Gramsci note, prison provides a lexicon of power and the execution is a display of the State's power over its subjects. But for Wilde, the performance also has a subversive purpose once it is conveyed to the one audience, the law-abiding citizens, who are denied direct access to it. This subversion occurs in the transformative nature of performance, where the prisoners literally change from the abject to the beatified.

46 Wilde, *The Ballad of Reading Gaol*, 844.
47 Ibid., 846.
48 Ibid., 844.

Richard Schechner argues that theatrical performance has its roots in religious ritual, not necessarily the medieval rituals of the Mystery plays, but the more interactive shamanistic rituals of tribal populations. For Schechner, the act of performance itself is an alternate, non-textual system of meaning which uses prescribed actions as codes. The primary purpose of this system is transformative. Schechner writes,

> Transformations in theatre occur in three different places, and at three different levels: (1) in the drama, that is, the story; (2) in the performers whose special task it is to temporarily undergo a *rearrangement* of their body/mind; (3) in the audience where changes may either be temporary (entertainment) or permanent (ritual).[49]

Rather than seeing any performance, whether a ritual or a theatrical event, as a set of repeated actions, or as the enactment of the same narrative every time it is performed, subtle changes in meaning occur in the performers' bodies and in the receptions of different audiences.

This is one of the reasons Wilde emphasizes both the repeated movements and the spectacle of prison life. Echoing, as Christopher Nassaar has pointed out, Dante's circular levels of Hell, the prisoners are seen walking in circles in the courtyard.[50] Wilde renders each aspect of the prisoners' daily lives as a series of mindless repetitions, 'where all but Lust is turned to dust / in humanity's machine.'[51] Essentially, the prison strips its inmates of their humanity – their individuality, as Wilde sees it – by positioning them as actors in a never-changing pantomime, or a 'merry masquerade,' as

49 Schechner. *Essays on Performance Theory*, 123.

50 Christopher S. Nassaar. 'Wilde's "The Ballad of Reading Gaol."' *Explicator* 53, no. 3 (1995), 158–60.

51 Wilde, *The Ballad of Reading Gaol*, 858.

Wilde sarcastically calls it.[52] This is done, Wilde suggests, not for the prisoners' benefit who, as actors, do not have a wide perspective of the performance, but for an 'audience' who will have at best a mediated access to it, by either reading a newspaper or hearing a sermon. The performance does not work because it gets lost in translation; thus the question the poem asks is: what is the purpose of the uniforms, the silence, the mindless chores, and especially the roles of the prison officials, such as the Chaplain who twice a day leaves a 'little,' and unread, tract?[53]

But the performance, despite its failure in achieving its purported aims, succeeds in a less obvious fashion through the juxtaposition of allegorical figures onto the stark realism of the poem's prison images. The allegory is concentrated in the third section of the poem, where 'crooked shapes of Terror' shadow the prisoners and 'evil sprites' mock the prisoners' constant walking by dancing alongside them.[54] It is a jarring insertion into the poem because it takes the reader out of the naturalistic world and into the world of the theatre: Wilde uses words like 'marionettes' and 'masques' to describe these figures.[55] What is notable about these figures is that they do nothing but perform. Through their singing and their dancing of sarabands and rigadoons, their performing arabesques and pirouettes, they evoke that same repressed that the prisoners are supposed to embody. Schechner notes that

> performing is a public dreaming. Just as dream work combines the day's events with the dreamer's interior life creating a symbolic drama with an audience/participator of one, so public performance re-presents the fanta-

52 Ibid., 848.

53 Ibid.

54 Ibid., 850.

55 Ibid., 851.

> sies associates with blocked displays in gestures that are publicly acceptable. The display that can't happen ultimately happens, but in a traditional form.[56]

The use of the bodies in dance here represent the sexual crimes that have condemned both the wife-murdering Woolridge character and Wilde as well. And the song they sing, one stanza which ends with 'But he does not win who plays with Sin / In the secret House of Shame,' evokes Wilde's earlier poem 'The Harlot's House.'[57] The particularly sexual demonic forms contrast with the Christ-like figure of the condemned prisoner, who is never seen doing much of anything despite the fact that he is the object of the poem's gaze. The condemned man's function in the poem is simply to exist and to passively go to his execution. In this sense, he is a perfectly aesthetic figure, in that his import lies in the image he presents, not in any action he undertakes, much like Dorian Gray before his fall into corruption or Wilde's fairy tale character The Young King. As a dying man, the condemned prisoner is appropriately lifeless in character, his wistful glances at the sky signalling that he is not entirely present in the prison anymore.

The condemned man is Wilde's own negative ego ideal, the depiction of his comment to Lord Alfred Douglas in *De Profundis* about forgiveness:

> still as long as I remained free from all resentment, hardness, and scorn, I would be able to face life with much more calm and confidence than I would were my body in purple and fine linen, and the soul within it sick with hate.[58]

He represents what is to Wilde the only possible performance left after one has been reconstructed as the 'criminal,' the passive sufferer, someone who has no choice but to embrace and to fully re-

---

56 Schechner, *Essays on Performance Theory*, 179.

57 Wilde, *The Ballad of Reading Gaol*, 851.

58 Wilde, *De Profundis*, 731.

alize his abject nature. Hence the overdetermined nihilistic images in the final stanzas of the poem, from the anti-Tannhäuser reference of the condemned man's grave ('For three long years they will not sow / Or root or seedling there')[59] to descriptions of the prisoner as 'he of the swollen purple throat' and as 'a wretched man / Eaten by teeth of flame.'[60] There is no performance left for the dead prisoner; for Wilde, what is left to him and his fellow prisoners is a virtual death at the hands of the social order. As he writes in *De Profundis*,

> Suffering . . . is the means by which we exist, because it is the only means by which we become conscious of existing; and the remembrance of suffering in the past is necessary to us as the warrant, and evidence, of our continued identity.[61]

The Ballad of Reading Gaol serves as a model for Wilde's post-prison experience, not as a reminder that all the world's a stage, but that ultimately one's very self is based on the performance one is permitted to play.

59 Wilde, *The Ballad of Reading Gaol*, 855.

60 Ibid., 859, 860.

61 Ibid., 884.

Bibliography

Advertisement based on Sarony photograph. Oscar Wilde and His Literary Circle. William Andrews Clark Memorial Library, University of California, Los Angeles.

'Aesthetics v. Athletics.' 1881. Oscar Wilde and His Literary Circle. William Andrews Clark Memorial Library, University of California, Los Angeles. Wildeana 1.13.

Alkalay-Gut, Karen. 'The Thing He Loves: Murder as Aesthetic Experience in The Ballad of Reading Gaol.' *Victorian Poetry* 35, no. 3 (1997): 349–366.

Andrews, Alan. 'Horrible Flesh and Blood.' *Theatre Notebook* 36, no. 1 (1982): 34–35.

Arendt, Hannah. *The Origins of Totalitarianism.* New York: Harcourt Brace, 1975.

Arnold, Matthew. *The Complete Prose Works of Matthew Arnold*, vol. 3., edited by R.H. Super. Ann Arbor: University of Michigan Press, 1960–77.

Atkinson, Gordon. 'Oscar Wilde at Oxford.' *Cornhill Magazine* 66 (1929): 559–564.

Auerbach, Nina. *Ellen Terry: Player in Her Time.* Philadelphia: University of Pennsylvania Press, 1987.

Auslander, Philip. *From Acting to Performance: Essays in Modernism and Postmodernism.* New York: Routledge, 1997.

Austin, J.L. 'How to Do Things With Words.' In *Literary Theory: An Anthology*, edited by Julie Rivkin and Michael Ryan, 162–176. Malden, MA: Blackwell Publishing, 2004.

'The Bard of Beauty.' *Time*, April 1880. Oscar Wilde and His Literary Circle. William Andrews Clark Memorial Library, University of California, Los Angeles.

Bashford, Bruce. 'Oscar Wilde: His Criticism and His Critics.' *ELT* 20 (1977), 412–422.

Baudelaire, Charles. *The Painter of Modern Life and Other Essays*, edited and translated by Jonathan Mayne. London: Phaidon, 1964.

Beatty, Laura. *Lillie Langtry: Manners, Masks and Morals*. London: Chatto and Windus, 1999.

Belford, Barbara. *Oscar Wilde: A Certain Genius*. New York: Random House, 2000.

Bernhardt, Sarah. *My Double Life*, translated by Victoria Tietze Larson. 1907. Albany: State University of New York Press, 1999.

Booth, Michael R. *Theatre in the Victorian Age*. Cambridge: Cambridge University Press, 1991.

Brake, Laurel. *Subjugated Knowledges: Journalism, Gender and Literature in the Nineteenth Century*. New York: New York University Press, 1994.

Brandon, Ruth. *Being Divine: A Biography of Sarah Bernhardt*. London: Mandarin, 1992.

Bristow, Joseph. *Effeminate England: Homoerotic Writing After 1895*. New York: Columbia University Press, 1995.

— . 'Wilde, *Dorian Gray*, and Gross Indecency.' In *Sexual Sameness: Textual Differences in Lesbian and Gay Writing*, edited by Joseph Bristow, 44–63. London and New York: Routledge, 1992.

'The British Fungus and the *Wild* American Sunflowers.' *Harper's Weekly*, 1882. Oscar Wilde and His Literary Circle. William Andrews Clark Memorial Library, University of California, Los Angeles.

Brough, James. *The Prince and the Lily*. London: Hodder and Stoughton, 1975.

Brown, Julia Prewitt. *Cosmopolitan Criticism: Oscar Wilde's Philosophy of Art*. Charlottesville, VA, and London: University Press of Virginia, 1997.

Buckler, William E. 'Oscar Wilde's Aesthetic of the Self: Art as Imaginative Self-Realization in *De Profundis*.' *Biography* 12, no. 2 (1989): 95–115.

Bucknell, Brad. 'On "Seeing" Salome.' *ELH* 60, no. 2 (1993): 50--526.

Burdett, Osbert. *The Beardsley Period: An Essay in Perspective*. London: Bodley Head, 1925.

Burgess, Gilbert. 'A Talk with Mr. Oscar Wilde.' *The Sketch*, 9 January 1895.

Butler, Judith. *Bodies That Matter: On the Discursive Limits of 'Sex'*. New York: Routledge, 1993.

— . *Gender Trouble: Feminism and the Subversion of Identity*. New York: Routledge, 1990.

Butwin, Joseph. 'The Martyr Clown: Oscar Wilde in *De Profundis*.' *Victorian Newsletter* 42 (1972): 1–6.

Cantor, Paul A. 'Oscar Wilde: The Man of Soul Under Socialism.' In *Beauty and the Critic: Aesthetics in an Age of Cultural Studies*, edited by James Sonderholm, 74–93. Tuscaloosa, AL: University of Alabama Press, 1997.

Carlson, Marvin. *Performance: A Critical Introduction*. London: Routledge, 1996.

Clifford, William Kingdon. *Lectures and Essays*, vol.1, edited by Leslie Stephen and Frederick Pollock. London: Macmillan, 1879.

Cohen, Ed. *Talk on the Wilde Side: Toward a Genealogy of Discourse on Male Sexualities*. New York: Routledge, 1993.

— . 'Writing Gone Wilde: Homoerotic Desire in the Closet of Representation.' *PMLA* 102, no. 5 (1987): 801–813.

Currier, Nathaniel, and James Merritt Ives. 'The Aesthetic Craze.' 1882. Oscar Wilde and His Literary Circle. William Andrews Clark Memorial Library, University of California, Los Angeles.

The Daily Telegraph, 6 April 1895.

Danson, Lawrence. *Wilde's Intentions: The Artist in his Criticism*. Oxford: Clarendon Press, 1997.

Dijkstra, Bram. *Idols of Perversity: Fantasies of Feminine Evil in Fin-de-Siècle Culture*. New York: Oxford University Press, 1986.

Dollimore, Jonathan. *Sexual Dissidence: Augustine to Wilde, Freud to Foucault*. Oxford: Oxford University Press, 1991.

Dowling, Linda. *Hellenism and Homosexuality in Victorian Oxford*. Ithaca and London: Cornell University Press, 1994.

— . 'Walter Pater and the Matter of the Self.' In *Die Modernisierung des Ich: Studien zur Subjektkinstitution in der Ver- und Frühmoderne*, edited by Manfred Pfister, 64–73. Passau: Wissenschaftsverlag Richard Rothe, 1989.

Dudley, Ernest. *The Gilded Lily: The Life and Loves of the Fabulous Lillie Langtry*. London: Oldhams Press, 1958.

Du Maurier, George. 'Maudle on the Choice of a Profession.' *Punch*, 30 October 1880.

Duval, E.B. 'National Aesthetics.' 1882. Oscar Wilde and His Literary Circle. William Andrews Clark Memorial Library, University of California, Los Angeles.

Ellmann, Richard. *Oscar Wilde.* New York: Vintage, 1988.

Eltis, Sos. *Revising Wilde: Society and Subversion in the Plays of Oscar Wilde.* Oxford: Clarendon Press, 1996.

Ericksen, Donald H. *Oscar Wilde.* Boston: Twayne, 1977.

The Evening News, 9 March 1895.

—, 5 April 1895.

Fitch, Clyde. Letter to Oscar Wilde, 1889? Oscar Wilde and His Literary Circle. William Andrews Clark Memorial Library, University of California, Los Angeles.

Fortnightly Review, 1 May 1908.

Foucault, Michel. *Discipline and Punish: The Birth of the Prison*, translated by Alan Sheridan. New York: Vintage, 1995.

Freud, Sigmund. *Beyond the Pleasure Principle*, edited and translated by James Strachey. New York: Norton, 1961.

Gagnier, Regenia. '*De Profundis* as *Epistola: in Carcere et Vinculis*: A Materialist Reading of Oscar Wilde's Autobiography.' *Criticism* 26, no. 4 (1984): 335–354.

—. *Idylls of the Marketplace: Oscar Wilde and the Victorian Public.* Stanford: Stanford University Press, 1986.

—. 'The Law of Progress and the Ironies of Individualism in the Nineteenth Century.' *New Literary History* 31, no. 2 (2000): 315–336.

Ganz, Arthur. 'The Meaning of *The Importance of Being Earnest.*' *Modern Drama* 6, no. 1 (1963): 42–52.

Garelick, Rhonda K. *Rising Star: Dandyism, Gender, and Performance in the Fin de Siècle.* Princeton: Princeton University Press, 1998.

Gilbert, Elliott L. '"Tumult of Images": Wilde, Beardsley, and *Salome.*' *Victorian Studies* 26, no. 2 (1983): 133–159.

Goffman, Erving. *The Presentation of Self in Everyday Life.* Woodstock, NY: Overlook Press, 1973.

Gold, Arthur, and Sir Robert Fizdale. *The Divine Sarah: A Life of Sarah Bernhardt.* New York: Knopf, 1991.

Gramsci, Antonio. *Selections from the Prison Notebooks*, edited and translated by Quintin Hoare and Geoffrey Nowell Smith. London: Lawrence and Wishart, 1971.

Gregor, Ian. 'Comedy and Oscar Wilde.' In *Wilde: Comedies*, edited by William Tydeman, 111–126. London: Macmillan, 1982.

Heidegger, Martin. *Poetry, Language, Thought*, translated and introduction by Albert Hofstadter. New York: Harper Collins, 1971.

Holland, Vyvyan. *Son of Oscar Wilde.* London: Rupert Hart-Davis, 1954.

Humphreys, Kathryn. 'The Artistic Exchange: *Dorian Gray* at the *Sacred Fount.*' *Texas Studies in Literature and Language* 32, no. 4 (1990): 522–535.

Huxley, Thomas. *Hume.* 1878. London: Macmillan, 1902.

Hyde, H. Montgomery. *Oscar Wilde.* New York: Farrar, Straus and Giroux, 1975.

Illustrated London News, 12 January 1895.

The Illustrated Police Budget, 13 April 1895.

—, 1 June 1895.

Jackson, Russell. 'Horrible Flesh and Blood – A Rejoinder.' *Theatre Notebook* 37, no. 1 (1983): 29–31.

James, Henry. *The Scenic Art: Notes on Acting and the Drama 1872–1901*, edited by Allan Wade. New York: Hill and Wang, 1957.

Jowett, Benjamin. 'Introduction to "Theaetetus."' In *The Dialogues of Plato*, edited by Benjamin Jowett, vol. 4. 3rd ed., 1871. London: Oxford University Press, 1892.

Kohl, Norbert. *Oscar Wilde: The Works of a Conformist Rebel*, translated by David Henry Wilson. Cambridge: Cambridge University Press, 1989.

Kopelson, Kevin R. 'Wilde's Love-Deaths.' *Yale Journal of Criticism* 5, no. 3 (1992): 31–61.

Langtry, Lillie. *The Days I Knew.* New York: George H. Doran, 1925.

Lawler, Donald. 'The Revisions of *Dorian Gray.*' *Victorians Institute Journal* 3 (1974): 21–36.

Le Gallienne, Richard. *The Romantic '90s.* New York: Doubleday Page, 1926.

Lesjak, Carolyn. 'Utopia, Use, and the Everyday: Oscar Wilde and a New Economy of Pleasure.' *ELH* 67, no. 1 (2000): 179–204.

Lester, John A., Jr. *Journey Through Despair 1880–1914: Transformations in British Literary Culture.* Princeton: Princeton University Press, 1968.

Leverson, Ada. 'The Last First Night.' *New Criterion*, January 1926.

Lewis, Hanna B. 'Salome and Elektra: Sisters or Strangers.' *Orbis Litterarum* 31 (1976): 125–33.

Lewis, Lloyd, and Henry Justin Smith. *Oscar Wilde Discovers America [1882].* New York: Benjamin Blom, 1967.

Liebman, Sheldon W. 'Character Design in *The Picture of Dorian Gray.*' *Studies in the Novel* 31, no. 3 (1999): 296–316.

London Evening News, 25 May 1895.

London Times, 3 July 1879.

—, 13 December 1880.

—, 20 December 1883.

Losey, Jay. 'The Aesthetics of Exile: Wilde Transforming Dante in *Intentions* and *De Profundis.*' *ELT* 36, no. 4 (1993): 429–450.

Marcus, Steven. 'Conceptions of the Self in an Age of Progress.' In *Progress and Its Discontents*, edited by Gabriel A. Almond, Marvin Chodorow, and Roy Harvey Pearce, 431–48. Berkeley: University of California Press, 1982.

Meyer, Moe. 'Introduction: Reclaiming the Discourse of Camp.' In *The Politics and Poetics of Camp*, edited by Moe Meyer, 1–21. London: Routledge, 1994.

Mikhail, E.H., ed. *Oscar Wilde: Interviews and Recollections*, vol. 1. London: Macmillan, 1979.

—. 'Self-Revelation in *An Ideal Husband.*' *Modern Drama* 11, no. 2 (1968): 180–186.

Moers, Ellen. *The Dandy: Brummell to Beerbohm.* New York: Viking, 1960.

Morrison, Kristin. 'Horrible Flesh and Blood.' *Theatre Notebook* 35, no. 1 (1981): 7–9.

Nassaar, Christopher S. "Wilde's 'The Ballad of Reading Gaol.'" *Explicator* 53, no. 3 (1995): 158–160.

— . 'Wilde's *The Picture of Dorian Gray* and *Salome*.' *Explicator* 57, no. 1 (1988): 33–36.

Nathan, Leonard. 'The Ballads of Reading Gaol: At the Limits of the Lyric.' In *Critical Essays on Oscar Wilde*, edited by Regenia Gagnier, 213–222. New York: G.K. Hall, 1991.

Novitz, David. 'Art, Life and Reality.' *British Journal of Aesthetics* 30, no. 4 (1990), 301–310.

Nunokawa, Jeffrey. 'The Disappearance of the Homosexual in *The Picture of Dorian Gray*.' In *Professions of Desire: Lesbian and Gay Studies in Literature*, edited by George E. Haggerty and Bonnie Zimmerman, 183–190. New York: Modern Language Association, 1995.

'Oscar Wilde, the Apostle of Aestheticism. From a photograph by Sarony.' *Frank Leslie's Illustrated Newspaper*, Jan 21 1882. William Andrews Clark Memorial Library, Los Angeles, California.

Parker, Andrew, and Eve Kosofsky Sedgwick. 'Introduction to *Performativity and Performance*.' In *The Performance Studies Reader*, edited by Henry Bial, 167–174. New York: Routledge, 2004.

Pater, Walter. *The Renaissance: Studies in Art and Poetry. The 1893 Text*, edited by Donald L. Hill. Berkeley and Los Angeles: University of California Press, 1980.

Pearson, Hesketh. *Oscar Wilde: His Life and Wit.* New York: Harper and Brothers, 1946.

Peckham, Morse. 'What Did Lady Windermere Learn?' *College English* 18 (1956): 11–14.

Powell, Kerry. *Oscar Wilde and the Theatre of the 1890s.* Cambridge: Cambridge University Press, 1990.

Quigley, Austin E. 'Realism and Symbolism in Oscar Wilde's *Salomé*.' *Modern Drama* 37, no. 1 (1994): 104–119.

Raby, Peter, ed.. *The Cambridge Companion to Oscar Wilde.* Cambridge: Cambridge University Press, 1997.

Renan, Ernest. *The Life of Jesus.* London: Watts and Co., 1861.

'Reviews and Magazines,' *Scots Observer*, 5 July 1890.

Riquelme, J[ohn] P[aul]. 'Shalom/Solomon/*Salomé*: Modernism and Wilde's Aesthetic Politics.' *Centennial Review* 39, no. 3 (1995): 575–610.

Rosenfeld, M.H. 'Oscar Dear!' Oscar Wilde and His Literary Circle. William Andrews Clark Memorial Library, University of California, Los Angeles. Wildeana 5.3.B2.

Ruskin, John. *The Genius of John Ruskin: Selections from His Writings*, edited by John D. Rosenberg. New York: George Brazillier, 1963.

Sagoff, Mark. 'On the Aesthetic and Economic Value of Art.' In *Aesthetics*, edited by Susan Feagin and Patrick Maynard, 119–128. Oxford and New York: Oxford University Press, 1997.

San Juan, Epifanio, Jr. *The Art of Oscar Wilde*. Princeton: Princeton University Press, 1967.

Schechner, Richard. *Environmental Theater*. 2nd ed. New York: Applause, 1994.

—. *Essays on Performance Theory 1970–1976*. New York: Drama Book Specialists, 1977.

Schmidgall, Gary. *The Stranger Wilde: Interpreting Oscar*. New York: Dutton, 1994.

Shewan, Rodney. *Oscar Wilde: Art and Egotism*. London: Macmillan, 1977.

Sinfield, Alan. *The Wilde Century: Effeminacy, Oscar Wilde and the Queer Moment*. New York: Columbia University Press, 1994.

Smith, Elaine. 'Oscar Wilde's *The Picture of Dorian Gray*: A Decadent Portrait of Life in Art – or Art in Life.' *Publications of the Arkansas Philological Association* 19, no. 1 (1993): 23–31.

Spencer, Herbert. *The Study of Sociology*. 1873. New York: D. Appleton, 1896.

The Star, 3 April 1895.

States, Bert O. *Great Reckonings in Little Rooms: On the Phenomenology of Theater*. Berkeley: University of California Press, 1987.

Stokes, John. *Oscar Wilde: Myths, Miracles, and Imitations*. Cambridge: Cambridge University Press, 1996.

—, Michael Booth, and Susan Bassnett. *Bernhardt, Terry, Duse: The Actress in Her Time*. Cambridge: Cambridge University Press, 1988.

Sussman, Herbert. 'Criticism as Art: Form in Oscar Wilde's Critical Writings.' *Studies in Philology* 70 (1973): 108–122.

Theatre, 1 June 1893.

Thomas, Martine. 'Oscar Wilde's *Salome*: A Few "Fin de Siecle" Aspects.' *Cahiers victoriens et edouardiens* 36 (1992): 153–169.

Times, 17 February 1895.

Truth, 21 February 1895.

Turner, Victor. *Dramas, Fields, and Metaphors: Symbolic Action in Human Society*. Ithaca and London: Cornell University Press, 1974.

U.S. Census Bureau. 'Table 1. Nativity of the Population and Place of Birth of the Native Population: 1850 to 1990.' <http://www.census.gov/population/www/documentation/twps0029/tab01.html>.

Vanity Fair, 19 May 1877.

Von Eckhardt, Wolf, Sander L. Gilman, and J. Edward Chamberlin. *Oscar Wilde's London: A Scrapbook of Vices and Virtues 1890–1900*. Garden City, NY: Anchor Press, 1987.

Wallen, Jeffrey. 'Reflection and Self-Reflection: Narcissistic or Aesthetic Criticism?' *Texas Studies in Literature and Language* 34, no. 3 (1992): 301–322.

Walshe, Eibhar. '"Angels of Death": Wilde's Salome and Shaw's Saint Joan.' *Irish University Review* 27, no. 1 (1997): 24–32.

The West Middlesex Advertiser, 14 July 1883. Oscar Wilde and His Literary Circle. William Andrews Clark Memorial Library, University of California, Los Angeles.

Westminster Review, April 1892.

Wilde, Oscar. *The Artist as Critic: Critical Writings of Oscar Wilde*, edited by Richard Ellmann. Chicago: University of Chicago Press.

— . *The Complete Letters of Oscar Wilde*, edited by Merlin Holland and Rupert Hart-Davis. New York: Henry Holt, 2000.

— . *The Complete Works of Oscar Wilde*. New York: Barnes and Noble, 1994.

—. *The Importance of Being Earnest and Other Plays*, edited by Peter Raby. Oxford: Oxford University Press, 2008.

—. *Oscar Wilde's Oxford Notebooks: A Portrait of Mind in the Making*, edited and introduction by Philip E. Smith II and Michael S. Helfand. New York: Oxford University Press, 1989.

—. *The Picture of Dorian Gray*. 1890 and 1891 versions, edited by Donald L. Lawler. New York: Norton, 1988.

—. *The Soul of Man under Socialism and Selected Critical Prose*, edited by Linda Dowling. London: Penguin, 2001.

—. *The Uncollected Oscar Wilde*, edited by John Wyse Jackson. London: Fourth Estate Limited, 1995.

Willoughby, Guy. *Art and Christhood: The Aesthetics of Oscar Wilde*. Cranbury, NJ: Associated University Press, 1993.

World, 26 April 1893.

—, 20 February 1895.

Žižek, Slavoj. *The Sublime Object of Ideology*. London: Verso, 1989.

Kolibri 360 GmbH
Ferdinand-Jühlke-Straße 7
99095 Erfurt, Deutschland
produktsicherheit@kolibri360.de